Serghei Golunov

THE ELEPHANT IN THE ROOM

Corruption and Cheating in Russian Universities

ibidem-Verlag
Stuttgart

Bibliografische Information der Deutschen Nationalbibliothek
Die Deutsche Nationalbibliothek verzeichnet diese Publikation in der Deutschen Nationalbibliografie; detaillierte bibliografische Daten sind im Internet über http://dnb.d-nb.de abrufbar.

Bibliographic information published by the Deutsche Nationalbibliothek
Die Deutsche Nationalbibliothek lists this publication in the Deutsche Nationalbibliografie; detailed bibliographic data are available in the Internet at http://dnb.d-nb.de.

Cover picture: Banksy art exhibit "Barely Legal" in Los Angeles, 16 September 2006. The exhibition featured this live "elephant in a room," painted, which, according to leaflets handed out at the exhibition, was intended to draw attention to the issue of world poverty. Author: Bit Boy. Source: Wikimedia.commons. Licensed under CC BY 2.0.

∞

Gedruckt auf alterungsbeständigem, säurefreien Papier
Printed on acid-free paper

ISSN: 1614-3515

ISBN-13: 978-3-8382-0570-0

© *ibidem*-Verlag
Stuttgart 2014

Alle Rechte vorbehalten

Das Werk einschließlich aller seiner Teile ist urheberrechtlich geschützt. Jede Verwertung außerhalb der engen Grenzen des Urheberrechtsgesetzes ist ohne Zustimmung des Verlages unzulässig und strafbar. Dies gilt insbesondere für Vervielfältigungen, Übersetzungen, Mikroverfilmungen und elektronische Speicherformen sowie die Einspeicherung und Verarbeitung in elektronischen Systemen.

All rights reserved. No part of this publication may be reproduced, stored in or introduced into a retrieval system, or transmitted, in any form, or by any means (electronic, mechanical, photocopying, recording or otherwise) without the prior written permission of the publisher. Any person who does any unauthorized act in relation to this publication may be liable to criminal prosecution and civil claims for damages.

Printed in Germany

Soviet and Post-Soviet Politics and Society (SPPS) Vol. 132
ISSN 1614-3515

General Editor: Andreas Umland,
Kyiv-Mohyla Academy, umland@stanfordalumni.org

Commissioning Editor: Max Jakob Horstmann,
London, mjh@ibidem.eu

EDITORIAL COMMITTEE*

DOMESTIC & COMPARATIVE POLITICS
Prof. **Ellen Bos**, *Andrássy University of Budapest*
Dr. **Ingmar Bredies**, *FH Bund, Brühl*
Dr. **Andrey Kazantsev**, *MGIMO (U) MID RF, Moscow*
Dr. **Heiko Pleines**, *University of Bremen*
Prof. **Richard Sakwa**, *University of Kent at Canterbury*
Dr. **Sarah Whitmore**, *Oxford Brookes University*
Dr. **Harald Wydra**, *University of Cambridge*
SOCIETY, CLASS & ETHNICITY
Col. **David Glantz**, *"Journal of Slavic Military Studies"*
Dr. **Marlène Laruelle**, *George Washington University*
Dr. **Stephen Shulman**, *Southern Illinois University*
Prof. **Stefan Troebst**, *University of Leipzig*
POLITICAL ECONOMY & PUBLIC POLICY
Prof. em. **Marshall Goldman**, *Wellesley College, Mass.*
Dr. **Andreas Goldthau**, *Central European University*
Dr. **Robert Kravchuk**, *University of North Carolina*
Dr. **David Lane**, *University of Cambridge*
Dr. **Carol Leonard**, *University of Oxford*
Dr. **Maria Popova**, *McGill University, Montreal*

FOREIGN POLICY & INTERNATIONAL AFFAIRS
Dr. **Peter Duncan**, *University College London*
Dr. **Taras Kuzio**, *Johns Hopkins University*
Prof. **Gerhard Mangott**, *University of Innsbruck*
Dr. **Diana Schmidt-Pfister**, *University of Konstanz*
Dr. **Lisbeth Tarlow**, *Harvard University, Cambridge*
Dr. **Christian Wipperfürth**, *N-Ost Network, Berlin*
Dr. **William Zimmerman**, *University of Michigan*
HISTORY, CULTURE & THOUGHT
Dr. **Catherine Andreyev**, *University of Oxford*
Prof. **Mark Bassin**, *Södertörn University*
Prof. **Karsten Brüggemann**, *Tallinn University*
Dr. **Alexander Etkind**, *University of Cambridge*
Dr. **Gasan Gusejnov**, *Moscow State University*
Prof. em. **Walter Laqueur**, *Georgetown University*
Prof. **Leonid Luks**, *Catholic University of Eichstaett*
Dr. **Olga Malinova**, *Russian Academy of Sciences*
Prof. **Andrei Rogatchevski**, *University of Tromsø*
Dr. **Mark Tauger**, *West Virginia University*
Dr. **Stefan Wiederkehr**, *BBAW, Berlin*

ADVISORY BOARD*

Prof. **Dominique Arel**, *University of Ottawa*
Prof. **Jörg Baberowski**, *Humboldt University of Berlin*
Prof. **Margarita Balmaceda**, *Seton Hall University*
Dr. **John Barber**, *University of Cambridge*
Prof. **Timm Beichelt**, *European University Viadrina*
Dr. **Katrin Boeckh**, *University of Munich*
Prof. em. **Archie Brown**, *University of Oxford*
Dr. **Vyacheslav Bryukhovetsky**, *Kyiv-Mohyla Academy*
Prof. **Timothy Colton**, *Harvard University, Cambridge*
Prof. **Paul D'Anieri**, *University of Florida*
Dr. **Heike Dörrenbächer**, *DGO, Berlin*
Dr. **John Dunlop**, *Hoover Institution, Stanford, California*
Dr. **Sabine Fischer**, *SWP, Berlin*
Dr. **Geir Flikke**, *NUPI, Oslo*
Prof. **David Galbreath**, *University of Aberdeen*
Prof. **Alexander Galkin**, *Russian Academy of Sciences*
Prof. **Frank Golczewski**, *University of Hamburg*
Dr. **Nikolas Gvosdev**, *Naval War College, Newport, RI*
Prof. **Mark von Hagen**, *Arizona State University*
Dr. **Guido Hausmann**, *University of Freiburg i.Br.*
Prof. **Dale Herspring**, *Kansas State University*
Dr. **Stefani Hoffman**, *Hebrew University of Jerusalem*
Prof. **Mikhail Ilyin**, *MGIMO (U) MID RF, Moscow*
Prof. **Vladimir Kantor**, *Higher School of Economics*
Dr. **Ivan Katchanovski**, *University of Ottawa*
Prof. em. **Andrzej Korbonski**, *University of California*
Dr. **Iris Kempe**, *"Caucasus Analytical Digest"*
Prof. **Herbert Küpper**, *Institut für Ostrecht Regensburg*
Dr. **Rainer Lindner**, *CEEER, Berlin*
Dr. **Vladimir Malakhov**, *Russian Academy of Sciences*

Dr. **Luke March**, *University of Edinburgh*
Prof. **Michael McFaul**, *US Embassy at Moscow*
Prof. **Birgit Menzel**, *University of Mainz-Germersheim*
Prof. **Valery Mikhailenko**, *The Urals State University*
Prof. **Emil Pain**, *Higher School of Economics, Moscow*
Dr. **Oleg Podvintsev**, *Russian Academy of Sciences*
Prof. **Olga Popova**, *St. Petersburg State University*
Dr. **Alex Pravda**, *University of Oxford*
Dr. **Erik van Ree**, *University of Amsterdam*
Dr. **Joachim Rogall**, *Robert Bosch Foundation Stuttgart*
Prof. **Peter Rutland**, *Wesleyan University, Middletown*
Prof. **Marat Salikov**, *The Urals State Law Academy*
Dr. **Gwendolyn Sasse**, *University of Oxford*
Prof. **Jutta Scherrer**, *EHESS, Paris*
Prof. **Robert Service**, *University of Oxford*
Mr. **James Sherr**, *RIIA Chatham House London*
Dr. **Oxana Shevel**, *Tufts University, Medford*
Prof. **Eberhard Schneider**, *University of Siegen*
Prof. **Olexander Shnyrkov**, *Shevchenko University, Kyiv*
Prof. **Hans-Henning Schröder**, *SWP, Berlin*
Prof. **Yuri Shapoval**, *Ukrainian Academy of Sciences*
Prof. **Viktor Shnirelman**, *Russian Academy of Sciences*
Dr. **Lisa Sundstrom**, *University of British Columbia*
Dr. **Philip Walters**, *"Religion, State and Society", Oxford*
Prof. **Zenon Wasyliw**, *Ithaca College, New York State*
Dr. **Lucan Way**, *University of Toronto*
Dr. **Markus Wehner**, *"Frankfurter Allgemeine Zeitung"*
Dr. **Andrew Wilson**, *University College London*
Prof. **Jan Zielonka**, *University of Oxford*
Prof. **Andrei Zorin**, *University of Oxford*

* While the Editorial Committee and Advisory Board support the General Editor in the choice and improvement of manuscripts for publication, responsibility for remaining errors and misinterpretations in the series' volumes lies with the books' authors.

Soviet and Post-Soviet Politics and Society (SPPS)
ISSN 1614-3515

Founded in 2004 and refereed since 2007, SPPS makes available affordable English-, German-, and Russian-language studies on the history of the countries of the former Soviet bloc from the late Tsarist period to today. It publishes between 5 and 20 volumes per year and focuses on issues in transitions to and from democracy such as economic crisis, identity formation, civil society development, and constitutional reform in CEE and the NIS. SPPS also aims to highlight so far understudied themes in East European studies such as right-wing radicalism, religious life, higher education, or human rights protection. The authors and titles of all previously published volumes are listed at the end of this book. For a full description of the series and reviews of its books, see www.ibidem-verlag.de/red/spps.

Editorial correspondence & manuscripts should be sent to: Dr. Andreas Umland, DAAD, German Embassy, vul. Bohdana Khmelnitskoho 25, UA-01901 Kyiv, Ukraine. e-mail: umland@stanfordalumni.org

Business correspondence & review copy requests should be sent to: *ibidem* Press, Leuschnerstr. 40, 30457 Hannover, Germany; tel.: +49 511 2622200; fax: +49 511 2622201; spps@ibidem.eu.

Authors, reviewers, referees, and editors for (as well as all other persons sympathetic to) SPPS are invited to join its networks at www.facebook.com/group.php?gid=52638198614 www.linkedin.com/groups?about=&gid=103012 www.xing.com/net/spps-ibidem-verlag/

Recent Volumes

123 Nicole Krome
Russischer Netzwerkkapitalismus
Restrukturierungsprozesse in der Russischen Föderation am Beispiel des Luftfahrtunternehmens "Aviastar"
Mit einem Vorwort von Petra Stykow
ISBN 978-3-8382-0534-2

124 David R. Marples
'Our Glorious Past'
Lukashenka's Belarus and the Great Patriotic War
ISBN 978-3-8382-0574-8 (Paperback edition)
ISBN 978-3-8382-0675-2 (Hardcover edition)

125 Ulf Walther
Russlands "neuer Adel"
Die Macht des Geheimdienstes von Gorbatschow bis Putin
Mit einem Vorwort von Hans-Georg Wieck
ISBN 978-3-8382-0584-7

126 Simon Geissbühler (Hrsg.)
Kiew – Revolution 3.0
Der Euromaidan 2013/14 und die Zukunftsperspektiven der Ukraine
ISBN 978-3-8382-0581-6 (Paperback edition)
ISBN 978-3-8382-0681-3 (Hardcover edition)

127 Andrey Makarychev
Russia and the EU in a Multipolar World
Discourses, Identities, Norms
With a foreword by Klaus Segbers
ISBN 978-3-8382-0629-5

128 Roland Scharff
Kasachstan als postsowjetischer Wohlfahrtsstaat
Die Transformation des sozialen Schutzsystems
Mit einem Vorwort von Joachim Ahrens
ISBN 978-3-8382-0622-6

129 Katja Grupp
Bild Lücke Deutschland
Kaliningrader Studierende sprechen über Deutschland
Mit einem Vorwort von Martin Schulz
ISBN 978-3-8382-0552-6

130 Konstantin Sheiko, Stephen Brown
History as Therapy
Alternative History and Nationalist Imaginings in Russia, 1991-2014
ISBN 978-3-8382-0665-3

131 Elisa Kriza
Alexander Solzhenitsyn: Cold War Icon, Gulag Author, Russian Nationalist?
A Study of the Western Reception of his Literary Writings, Historical Interpretations, and Political Ideas
With a foreword by Andrei Rogatchevski
ISBN 978-3-8382-0589-2 (Paperback edition)
ISBN 978-3-8382-0690-5 (Hardcover edition)

To the "silent heroes" of the Russian higher education system: to those ordinary university teachers who managed to preserve their integrity despite low salaries, pressures from higher authorities, and other unfavourable circumstances.

TABLE OF CONTENTS

Acknowledgements		IX
Abbreviations and acronyms		XI
1	**Introduction**	15
	1.1. The problem	15
	1.2. Existing works on the topic	16
	1.3. The approach	19
	1.4. Book structure	20
2	**Vulnerabilities of the Russian higher education system**	23
	2.1. Russian higher education system at a glance	23
	2.2. Some key trends of the post-Soviet period	27
	2.3. Influence of the environment	41
	2.4. Conclusion	46
3	**Corruption and cheating practices**	49
	3.1. Conceptualisations	49
	3.2. Corruption	53
	3.3. Cheating	67
	3.4. Consequences	77
	3.5. Conclusion	79
4	**Counteraction efforts**	81
	4.1. Strategies and best practices	81
	4.2. Official efforts	86
	4.3. Academic and student activism	93
	4.4. International impact	102
	4.5. Conclusion	107

5	**Conclusions**		109
	5.1.	Roots and relative importance of malpractices	109
	5.2.	Damage from malpractice	111
	5.3.	Efficiency of counteraction measures	112
	5.4.	Recommendations	114

Index   119

ACKNOWLEDGEMENTS

I am extremely grateful to the Institute of Government and Politics and the Centre for EU-Russian Studies at the University of Tartu for supporting this research. This support gave me an opportunity to concentrate on writing this book and to take a funded trip to work in the Russian State Library, Moscow.

As a non-native English writer I am also deeply thankful to Dr. Jolyon Dodgson for proofreading the book.

Volgograd, June 2014

Serghei Golunov

ABBREVIATIONS AND ACRONYMS

C.Sc.	Candidate of Sciences (academic degree)
D.Sc.	Doctor of Sciences (academic degree)
EHEA	European Higher Education Area
MES	Ministry of Education and Science, of the Russian Federation
MGIMO	*Moskovskii gosudarstvennyi institut mezhdunarodnykh otnoshenii* (Moscow State Institute of International Relations)
MSPU	Moscow State Pedagogical University
MSU	Moscow State University
Rosobrnadzor	*Federal'naia sluzhba po nadzoru v sfere obrazovaniia i nauki* (Federal Service of Supervision in the Sphere of Education and Science), of the Russian Federation
RANEPA	Russian Presidential Academy of National Economy and Public Administration
RAS	Russian Academy of Sciences
SPSU	St Petersburg State University
USE	Unified State Exam
VAK	*Vysshaia attestatsionnaia komissiia* (Higher Attestation Commission), of the Russian Federation

1 INTRODUCTION

1.1. The problem

Along with several other countries, Russia is often mentioned when discussing where corruption and other malpractices in education are widespread[1]. It is commonplace to argue that higher education is a very corrupted sphere in Russia. According to the results of an opinion poll held in 2011 by the Public Opinion Foundation, universities were ranked third in the list of everyday corruption after drivers' relations with car inspectors and child care[2]. Corruption, traditionally understood as an abuse of power for obtaining private gain[3], is not the only kind of malpractice that is pervasive in Russian higher education: indeed, various forms of cheating (such as plagiarism, cribbing, and receiving unauthorised hints during exams, etc.) are probably even more widespread than bribery, clientelism, embezzlement, or shadow paybacks.

It should be specifically stressed that not everything in the Russian higher education system is corrupt: the government takes some measures periodically, some universities pursue more consistent anti-corruption and anti-cheating policies than others, and, not least, there are still many principled teachers and students who avoid resorting to malpractices. Yet, as is argued in this book, the overall pervasiveness of malpractice is so great that it can lead to disastrous consequences, such as the devaluation of diplomas, the prevalence of corruption and dishonest behaviour in the younger generation, degradation of academic integrity, and the underfunding of crucially important education and research activities, etc. The current measures, taken against corruption and cheating by federal agencies and universities, are not suffi-

---

1 See for example: David Chapman, "Corruption and the Education Sector," *USAID* (2002), http://pdf.usaid.gov/pdf_docs/PNACT874.pdf (as of 2 May 2014).
2 "Bytovaia korruptsia v Rossii," *FOM,* 15 June 2011, http://http://fom.ru/obshchestvo/138 (as of 2 May 2014).
3 Jacques Hallak and Muriel Poisson, (2007) *Corrupt Schools, Corrupt Universities: What Can Be Done?* (Paris: International Institute for Educational Planning, 2007), 29.

cient; thus, the question "what should be done to combat malpractice more efficiently?" lies at the core of the current research.

It is worth mentioning that I had a strong personal motivation for conducting this research. I worked in an average provincial university for more than ten years, and witnessed many instances of malpractice personally and heard even more about them from my colleagues. I never took bribes (though I was offered them sometimes), but unfortunately was not always impeccable in terms of academic integrity: in particular, I sometimes gave undeservedly high marks to some well-connected students, yielding to the pressure of higher authorities, though there were some colleagues who had enough courage not to do it. In the last years of my employment in the Russian higher education system I faced plagiarism more and more often: on average about written work I checked contained large blocks of plagiarised text; thus, my work checking students' texts became increasingly mechanical and decreasingly meaningful. Even worse, I (and some of my colleagues also) started to be regularly pressurised by higher authorities who required high marks to be given for evidently plagiarised works[4]. It were cases of this kind that finally prompted me to try to obtain revenge not on specific people but on the entire vicious system. Thus, I decided to start policy-oriented research on malpractice in Russian higher education, and this finally resulted in the writing of this book.

1.2. Existing works on the topic

Internationally, corruption in education (including higher education) is considered in a relatively large number of scholarly works. However, the number of works trying to conceptualise the worldwide experience is relatively small. In this respect, publications that resulted from the International Institute for Educational Planning's research project "Ethics and Corruption in Education" and

---

[4] At least twice when I was forced to give undeservedly high marks I found no better solution than to give good marks to all students irrespectively of their performance so as not to give well-connected students any advantage.

especially the Hallack and Poisson book[5] should be mentioned. Another notable work is a volume edited by Heyneman[6]. Some other relevant works, such as Eckstein's paper dealing with academic cheating[7] as well as Heyneman, Anderson, and Nuraliyeva's article focusing on the cost of corruption[8] also proved to be especially useful in the course of the current research.

Though corruption in Russian higher education is sometimes considered as a too hackneyed subject, the number of fundamental works related to this topic is a very small. Leontieva's D.Sc. thesis[9] should be mentioned first of all, but it has a somewhat broader focus, as the range of informal practices includes not only corruption and cheating but also legitimate and semi-legitimate practices. There are also a larger number of articles conceptualising one or several key aspects of corruption in Russian higher education: marginalising the status of university teachers and commodifying the demand for diplomas[10], rapidly developing corruption culture[11], and legal treatment of bribery in universities[12], etc.

---

5   Hallak and Poisson, *Corrupt Schools*.
6   Stephen H. Heyneman (ed.) *Buying your way into Heaven: Education and Corruption in International Perspectivo*, (Rotterdam and Taipei: Sense Publishers, 2009).
7   Max Eckstein, *Combating academic fraud: Towards a culture of integrity* (Paris: International Institute for Educational Planning, 2003).
8   Stephen H. Heyneman, Kathryn Anderson, and Nazym Nuraliyeva, "The Cost of Corruption in Higher Education," *Comparative Education Review* 52:1 (2008): 22.
9   El'vira Leontieva, *Institutsionalizatsia neformal'nyh praktik v sfere vysshego obrazovania* [Doctor of Sociological Sciences' Dissertation] (Khabarovsk: Pacific National University, 2010).
10   Oleg Leibovich and Natalia Shushkova, "Na semi vetrah: institut vysshego obrazovania v postsovetskuyu epohum," *Zhurnal sotsiologii i sotsial'noy antropologii* VII:1 (2004); Piotr Orekhovskiy, "Teoria neiavnogo kontrakta" *Polit.ru,* 11 May 2011, http://polit.ru/article/2011/05/11/innov/ (as of 2 May 2014); Natalia Shushkova, Oleg Leibovich, " 'Hochesh' sdat' ekzamen na piat'?...'," *Otechestvennye zapiski* 47:2 (2012), http://magazines.russ.ru/oz/2012/2/sh24.html (as of 21 February 2014).
11   Vladimir Rimskii, "Sposobstvuet li sistema vysshego obrazovania rasprostraneniu korruptsii v Rossii," *Terra economicus* 8:3 (2010); Shushkova and Leibovich, " 'Hochesh' sdat' ekzamen na piat'?..."
12   Gennadiy Morozov, "Korruptsiya v obrazovanii: mify i realii normativno-pravovogo haraktera,' *Pedagogicheskoya obrazovaniye Rossii* 2 (2010): 149-159.

There are a lot of publicistic and blog entries written by those scholars who focused on individual malpractices: plagiarism[13], procurement and competition machinations[14], and exam-related machinations[15], etc. Many of these articles have been published in the *Troitskii variant*, which is a newspaper established as an informal initiative of academic activists.

Finally, there is one more kind of academic and publicistic entries that are written by scholars and these deal with those factors and trends that indirectly create a breeding ground for malpractice: massivisation[16], overbureaucratisation[17], and authoritarianism of university management systems[18], etc.

Thus, while there is a relatively large number of scholarly and publicistic works devoted to corruption and cheating in Russian higher education, there is a need for a large policy-oriented study that would conceptualise malpractice, evaluate current achievements of governmental and non-governmental

---

13 See for example: Ivan Kotliarov and Iurii Brumshtein, "Studencheskii plagiat: vlianie na intellektual'nuiu i informatsionnuiu bezopasnost' regionov," *Informatsionnaia bezopasnost' regionov* 1 (2012); Mefodii Volikhamov, "MGU i Dissergeit: opasnye sviazi," *Troitskii variant* 178 (2014), http://trv-science.ru/2014/02/25/mgu-i-dissergejjt-opasnye-svyazi/ (as of 10 April 2014); Vladimir Volkhonskii, "Pokolenie plagiata," *Troitskii variant* 124 (2013), http://trv-science.ru/2013/03/12/pokolenie-plagiata/ (as of 10 April 2014).
14 See for example: Aleksei Krushel'nitskii, "Pilite, Shura, pilite," *Troitskii variant* 68 (2010), http://trv-science.ru/2010/12/07/pilite-shura-pilite/ (as of 10 April 2010); Yevgeniy Onishchenko, "FTsP: konkursy i 'konkursy'," *Troitskii variant* 79 (2011), http://trv-science.ru/2011/05/24/fcp-konkursy-i-konkursy/ (as of 12 March 2014); Yevgeniy Onishchenko, "Kormlenie kak sistema," *Troitskiy variant* 35 (2009), http://trv-science.ru/2009/08/18/kormlenie-kak-sistema/ (as of 12 March 2014).
15 See for example: Leonid Ashkinazi, Maria Grishkina, and Svetlana Ivanova, "Utechka-test," Troitskii variant 131 (2013), http://trv-science.ru/2013/06/18/utechka-test/ (as of 10 April 2014).
16 Girsh Khanin, "Vysshee obrazovanie i sovetskoye obschestvo," *EKO* 8-9 (2008), http://www.econom.nsc.ru/eco/arhiv/ReadStatiy/2008_09/Hanin/index.htm#23/ (as of 5 January 2014).
17 See for example: Leonid Bliakher, "O vnutrennei biurokratii v vuzakh i ne tol'ko v vuzakh," *Livejournal*, 12 September 2012, http://lenya.livejournal.com/240801.html (as of 13 January 2014); Ivan Kurilla, "Kriterii otsenki: chitaia interviu Yaroslava Kuz'minova," *Troitskiy variant* 121 (2013), http://trv-science.ru/2013/01/29/kriterii-ocenki-chitaya-intervyu-yaroslava-kuzminova (as of 13 January 2014).
18 See for example: Vladimir Volkhonskii, "Piatiletka rektora Kropachëva," Troitskii variant 125 (2013), http://trv-science.ru/2013/03/26/pyatiletka-rektora-kropacheva/ (as of 10 April 2014).

actors trying to combatting the malpractice, and take into account the relevant international experience. I hope that this book could be considered a modest contribution to the research in this direction.

1.3. The approach

This book is primarily policy oriented. While I make an attempt to conceptualise the set of factors creating a breeding ground for malpractice, the main focus is related to examining the prevalence of malpractice, evaluating the efficiency of measures taken by various kinds of actors to combat it, and on proposing new measures aimed at improving this efficiency. The proposed measures take into account international experience of combatting corruption and fraud in the education sphere.

While analysing trends related to corruption and cheating, I had to rely largely on anecdotal evidence (news and stories told to me by my colleagues), my personal experience, and those online discussions I had with academic activists, e.g. with activists from the anti-plagiarism Dissernet network. Apart from this, I also analysed hundreds of biographies of Russian top officials and politicians as well as the principals of Russian universities, with the focus primarily on evaluating the circumstances in which they defended their doctoral theses[19].

In the course of writing this book I had to refer to accusations that, though being reasoned and not properly responded to, cannot be considered as clearly proven. For instance, an accusation of plagiarism, even if based on the comparison of two coinciding pieces of texts (provided that the text of an accused person was written later), can be considered to be not sufficiently grounded as literally coincided phrases theoretically can be commonly used by many and have no clear primary source, or can be plagiarised from some accused person's even earlier work. Taking also into account that the purpose of my book is not in identifying specific persons or institutions but rather in analysing common trends; I tried to minimise references to not explicitly

---

19 For greater detail see the section 3.3.

proven accusations in the main text while providing references to this kind of cases in the footnotes.

Moreover, as a Russian citizen, I should be cautious while using the very term "plagiarism" with respect to specific cases. As will be mentioned in the third part, according to the Russian Criminal Code, an accusation of plagiarism is an accusation of a crime that can easily be considered as ungrounded (and thus qualify as libel) by Russian courts even if the considered texts evidently coincide. For this reason, I deliberately use substitute wordings (such as "illegitimate textual borrowings") in many of these cases when specific accusations of plagiarism are considered.

1.4. Book structure

The current part characterises the scope of the problem, describes the range of existing works on the topic, and outlines the author's general approach and the approach towards covering some specific sensitive issues.

The second part, after describing the key features of the Russian higher education system, examines the negative trends of its development that created a breeding ground for various malpractices. Among such trends are massivisation, commercialisation, overbureaucratisation, growing authoritarianism of university management combined with reduction in the autonomy of universities' self-governance, and marginalisation of the position of ordinary university teachers. Apart from this, the role of the external environment in provoking malpractice in the Russian higher education system is also considered.

The third part focuses on corruption and cheating practices. In the beginning I consider some issues related to their conceptualisation, including the problem of delimitation between corruption and cheating. In the subsequent two sections I then examine specific kinds of corruption and cheating practices. After this I consider the consequences that the prevalence of malpractices entails both for the Russian higher education system and also for Russian society.

The fourth part assesses the measures taken to combat these malpractices. First, it examines the worldwide experience of fighting corruption and cheating. Second, it evaluates the relevant efforts taken by official Russian actors: the Ministry of Education and Science, and individual universities, etc. Third, it considers the efforts of non-governmental actors, especially the recently emerged movement for revealing dissertation fraud. Fourth, it focuses on the actual and potential influence of international actors and institutions, such as inter-university partnerships, international agreements, and global university ratings.

In the concluding chapter I summarise and analyse the previous findings and offer some recommendations on what should be done to combat malpractice in the Russian higher education system more effectively.

2 VULNERABILITIES OF THE RUSSIAN HIGHER EDUCATION SYSTEM

The malpractices that are pervasive in the Russian higher education system are largely a by-product of the system's development during the Soviet and especially post-Soviet periods. Though the history of Russian higher education began at the end of the 17th century, it was only during the time of the USSR that the majority of current universities were founded and the bulk of present-day management norms and practices were introduced. In the post-Soviet period the Russian higher education system experienced a dramatic transformation, including such processes as commercialisation, de-ideologisation, and impressive extensive growth.

Taking these considerations into account, I examine in this chapter first the key features of the higher education system, including its structure and management. After that I consider those key trends of the system's development in the Soviet and post-Soviet periods that created favourable ground for corruption and cheating. As the range of such trends is not caused just by internal processes within the higher education system, I focus finally on some relevant features of the system's interaction with social, political, and information environments.

2.1. Russian higher education system at a glance

Despite the negative influence of the "demographic hole" of the post-Soviet period, the Russian higher education system remains one of the largest in the world, being in the top five countries[20] both by the number of universities[21]

---

20 It would make no sense to specify Russian universities' positions in the corresponding rankings precisely as (it will be shown in this paragraph) the situation changes very dynamically.
21 "Countries Arranged by Number of Universities in Top Ranks," *Ranking Web of Universities,* 2013, http://www.webometrics.info/en/node/54 (as of 23 December 2013).

and by the number of university students[22]. As of 2012, some 6 million students were enrolled in 2.65 thousand universities: more than 5 million in 1.38 thousand state universities and the remaining 1.27 million in private universities. These students were taught by more than 271 thousand university teachers[23]. It should be taken into account that the number of Russian universities and their students are diminishing because of both an unfavourable demographic situation and current governmental policy aimed at reducing the number of universities and merging some of them.

The top national specialised agency supervising the Russian education system is the Ministry of Education and Science (MES). The key responsibilities of the MES include certification of universities and individual academics, monitoring of universities' key activities, elaborating and developing educational standards, strategic planning, and managing universities directly subordinated to the MES[24]. Among the bodies subordinated to the MES, Federal Service of Supervision in the Sphere of Education and Science (*Rosobrnadzor*) and the Higher Attestation Commission VAK perform especially important functions in light of the current research: the former is responsible for, among other matters, certification of universities and (together with local authorities) control over the Unified State Exam (USE)[25]; while, the latter is responsible for certification of universities' dissertation councils and for awarding the D.Sc. degree[26] as well as the academic ranks of Docent and Professor.

---

22 "Enrolment by Level of Education," *UNESCO Institute for Statistics*, 2013, http://data.uis.unesco.org/Index.aspx?queryid=93 (as of 23 December 2013).

23 "Minobrnauki: Obuchenie v vuzah v novom uchebnom godu nachnut 6 mln studentov," *RBK*, 30 August 2013, http://www.rbc.ru/rbcfreenews/20130830175059.shtml (as of 23 December 2013).

24 "Postanovlenie Pravitel'stva Rossiiskoi Federatsii ot 3 iunia 2013 g. no 466 g. Moskva, 'Ob utverzhdenii polozheniia o Ministerstve obrazovaniia i nauki Rossiiskoi Federatsii'," *Rossiiskaia gazeta*, 10 June 2013, http://www.rg.ru/2013/06/10/minobr-site-dok.
html (as of 23 December 2013).

25 Unified State Exam is a set of school-leaving exams, the scores from which serve as the main admission criterion for enrollment in universities.

26 Doctor of Sciences (D.Sc.) is the highest academic degree in Russia approximately equivalent to French or German Habilitation and formally awarded by the VAK (universities just recommend the VAK to award this degree). A lower academic degree of

MES has different powers towards Russian higher education institutions (universities, institutes, and academies, etc.[27]) of various kinds. It has the widest range of powers towards those universities that are directly subordinated to it: not only certifying these universities and individual programmes but also seriously influencing such universities' management by appointing acting principals, vetoing candidates for a principal's position, confirming the results of principals' elections, and by dismissing such principals on some grounds. At the same time, the MES has lesser powers towards universities controlled by other stakeholders (by higher federal authorities, provincial or municipal authorities, other governmental agencies[28], or private persons), which are related to still certifying and monitoring such institutions but not significantly influencing their governance.

As mentioned above, there are 2.65 thousand higher education institutions, many of which are autonomous branches subordinated to other higher education institutions[29]. In the 2000s and 2010s several universities were assigned the status of "federal university" that certifies an especially high quality of teaching and research within these institutions[30]. By the end of 2013 there were also 29 national research universities, which were selected on the basis

---

the Candidate of Sciences (C.Sc.—approximately equivalent to the Ph.D. degree) is formally awarded by universities' dissertation councils. See: "Polozheniye o Vysshei attestatsionnoi komissii pri Ministerstve obrazovaniya I nauki Rossiiskoy Federatsii," Vysshaya attestatsionnaya komissiya (VAK), http://vak.ed.gov.ru/ru/about/position/ (as of 25 December 2013).

27 For brevity's sake I will hereafter use the term "university" to denote all these kinds of higher education institutions.

28 Among those agencies that fund many universities, academies, and institutes and control their management, are the Defense Ministry, the Ministry of the Interior, the Ministry of Agriculture, and the Ministry for Culture, etc.

29 Russian Presidential Academy of National Economy and Public Administration (RANEPA) is distinguished by an especially large number of regional autonomous branches (68), some of which were independent academies and institutes before merging with RANEPA.

30 As of the end of 2013 there were nine universities of this kind in Russia, viz.: Baltic Federal University (Kaliningrad), Far Eastern Federal University (Vladivostok), Kazan (Volga Region) Federal University, North Caucasian Federal University (Stavropol), North-Eastern Federal University (Yakutsk), Northern (Arctic) Federal University (Arkhangelsk), Siberian Federal University (Krasnoyarsk), Southern Federal University (Rostov-on-Don), and Ural Federal University (Yekaterinburg).

of national competitions as universities capable of combining high-quality research with teaching. Federal and national universities obtain increased governmental funding and have some special privileges, such as the right to develop and use their own educational standards, while other universities should use the standards of the MES. At the same time, the federal universities' governance systems are less autonomous than the governance systems of the majority of other state universities as their rectors are not elected by their academic councils but appointed by the president of the Russian Federation (for Moscow State University and St. Petersburg State University) or by the federal government (for other federal universities).

Universities themselves are headed by principals, who are usually called rectors, directors, or (in military or paramilitary institutions) chiefs[31]. In some cases principals are elected by special assemblies (formed from representatives of a given university's staff and students) while in other cases they are appointed by higher authorities. Universities' governing bodies also include vice rectors and chief accountants. Many universities also have the position of president, but this position being nominally of equal level to the rector's post is mainly just ceremonial. The supreme representative body of a university is an academic council, consisting of a rector, vice rectors, heads of institutes and departments, prominent scholars, and representatives of students. Academic councils make decisions on key questions of a university's functioning and strategic development as well as recommend MES to award the rank of docent or professor to a university's employees, etc. The internal structure of universities usually consists of institutes (typically called *fakul'tety* and headed by deans) and departments (typically called *kafedry*).

The hierarchy of faculty positions in Russian universities typically includes the following positions: *assistent* (teaching assistant), *starshii prepodavatel'* (assistant professor), *dotsent* (docent, associate professor), and *professor* (full professor). There are also similar lifetime academic ranks of *dotsent* and *professor* awarded by the VAK to those who meet specific qualification requirements.

---

31 Hereafter the word 'rector' will be used to denote all kinds of heads of higher education institutions.

Like the majority of other countries, Russia now has a two-tier system: first-level graduates obtain the bachelor's degree while the second-level graduates obtain the master's (magister's) degree. At the same time, the specialist degree (which was the only graduate degree in the Soviet times), awarded to those graduates who successfully finish at least a five-year full time study programme, still also exists. The vast majority of students entering bachelor or specialist programmes after finishing secondary school have to get a sufficient score on the USE.

There are also two levels of post-graduate academic degrees—C.Sc. (roughly equivalent to the Ph.D. degree) and D.Sc. (approximately equivalent to the Habilitation in some EU countries) that are typically awarding for defending a thesis, provided that a candidate also meets some other qualification requirements (such as publishing a sufficient number of articles in eligible journals mentioned in the so-called "list of the VAK"). To qualify for defending a C.Sc. thesis a candidate should apart from publishing a smaller number of articles in journals included on the "list of the VAK" also pass three exams, the assortment of which depends on the field of the thesis. The majority of candidates for the C.Sc. degree finish post-graduate training programmes (*aspirantura*).

It should be noted that in the post-Soviet period the Russian system of higher education has been undergoing dramatic changes that have affected both its structure and the number of universities, academics, and students. Those trends that are important in light of the current study will be considered in the next section.

2.2. Some key system trends of the post-Soviet period

Throughout its post-Soviet history the Russian higher education system has periodically experienced shock changes, a large part of which were caused by uncontrolled social, economic, and political processes. Some of the changes greatly (and for the most part negatively) affected the system's capability to resist corruption and cheating. Among the trends in Russian higher education's development, which have particularly great impacts on its capability, have been massivisation and commercialisation, bureaucratisation of the educational process and growing authoritarianism in higher education management, and marginalisation of the university teachers' status. In the following I will consider these trends in more detail.

Massivisation

This process is rooted in the trends of the Soviet past. While in pre-revolutionary Russian universities higher education was largely elitist and the number of students in the Russian empire (including the territory of the contemporary Poland) in 1914 was only some 127 thousand, by the end of the 1920s the number of students in the USSR was already some 272 thousand, in 1932 it was 504 thousand, in 1940 it was 812 thousand, in 1956 it was 2.0 million, and in 1975 it was 4.9 million. The number of universities grew until the 1930s (105 in 1915, 148 in 1927, and 832 in 1932) but later remained relatively stable (between 800 and 900, more than 400 of which were situated in the territory of the current Russian Federation)[32].

Such a quick development, which was caused by the needs of economic modernisation and by democratisation of public access to higher education, in the most cases was not supported by adequate infrastructure or a suitable number of highly-qualified academic staff, especially in the 1920s and 1930s: especially taking into account the systematic repressions by the Soviet regime against many of those "ideologically suspicious" academics who worked previously in universities of the Russian empire. Instead, the selection criteria for potential academics were simplified radically: mainly due to the abolishment in 1918 of academic degrees and ranks by the Soviet government,

---

32 Boris Mironov, *Istoria v tsifrah* (Leningrad: Nauka, 1991), 136; Narodnoe hoziaystvo SSSR v Velikoy Otechestvennoy voyne 1941-1945 gg. Statisticheskiy sbornik (Moscow: Informatsionno-izdatel'skiy tsentr, 1990), http://istmat.info/node/374 (as of 25 December 2013); *Narodnoe hoziaystvo SSSR v 1956 g. (Statisticheskiy sbornik)* (Moscow: Gosudarstvennoe statisticheskoe izdatel'stvo, 1956), *http://istmat.info/node/ 17165* (as of 25 December 2013); "SSSR. Narodnoe obrazovanie", *Bol'shaia sovetskaia entsiklopediia,* http://dic.academic.ru/dic.nsf/bse/129062/%D0%A1%D0%A1%D0%A1%D0%A0 (as of 25 December 2013).

which were only restored in 1934. Similarly, the admission barriers for potential students were lowered dramatically: specifically, from 1918 until the second half of the 1920s individuals with any educational background, but preferentially with proletarian or peasant pauper social background, had a right to enter universities without passing entrance examinations. No wonder that the quality of control over the education process was also decreased significantly, as teachers during the Soviet period were oftentimes discouraged by higher authorities from being strict with their students. This trend was described by a known Russian writer Aleksandr Solzhenitsyn in his novel "In the First Circle"[33]:

> It suited Simochka very well that no one expected her to show any competence in her special field. Like many of her girl-friends there, she had not learned anything at her Institute—this for many reasons. The girls had done very little maths or physics at school. In their final years it had come to their ears that the headmaster was always reprimanding teachers for failing too many students, and they realized that they would scrape through even if they knew nothing. As a result, when the time came to go to university they were completely lost in the jungle of mathematics and radiotechnology—and very often they had no time at all for study...
> When the examinations came, Simoohka, like the other girls, wrote cribs, hid them in her clothes, smuggled them in and took them out and unfolded them at the right moment, so, that they looked like legitimate sheets of rough work. The ignoramuses could easily have been shown up if the examiners had asked enough questions at the orals, but the teachers themselves were overworked—what with committees, meetings and writing various memoranda and reports for the Dean and the Rector. Failing their students meant extra work examining them a second time. Besides, if their students failed, the teachers suffered, just like factory workers turning out defective goods—on the well-known principle that there are no bad pupils, only bad teachers. No wonder that they didn't try to catch their students out but did their best to get them through as quickly as possible and with the highest possible marks.

---

33 Alexander Solzhenitsyn, *The First Circle*, trans. Michael Glenny (London: Collins, 1970), 38-39.

Overall, assessing the development of Soviet higher education in the 1920s-30s, Girsh Khanin argues that the quantitative growth, unprecedented on a worldwide scale, was accompanied by an equally unprecedented degradation of quality, and that newly established Soviet universities could be rather matched with secondary technical schools. At the same time, the reforms of the mentioned period dramatically increased public access to higher education and greatly contributed to the impressive modernisation of Soviet economics[34].

The next wave of massivisation of higher education followed in the 1950s-70s: as was shown above, the number of students increased almost 2.5 times between 1956 and 1975, which was largely achieved due to a rapid increase in the number of students enrolled in evening and distance courses. That time it led to not only decreasing the quality of education in some fields (especially in social sciences) but also overproduction and devaluation of the importance of some categories of specialists, such as engineers[35].

Ironically, after the collapse of the USSR, Russian higher education experienced an almost as impressive wave of massivisation as in the 1920s-30s[36], and this happened despite the severe economic crisis of the 1990s. While in 1994 the number of students was 2.6 million, in 2001 it was already 5.4 million[37] and in 2008 it reached its peak of 7.5 million[38]. The number of universities grew at an even a higher rate: in 1990 there were just 514 and in 2013 already 2649[39].

---

34 Khanin, "Vysshee obrazovanie."
35 Khanin, "Vysshee obrazovanie;" Sergei Volkov, "Sotsial'nyi status intellektual'nogo sloya v XXI veke: tendentsii i perspektivy," http://swolkov.org/publ/03-1.htm (as of 26 December 2013).
36 Some researchers draw an explicit parallel between the "massivisation waves" of the 1920s-1930s and the 1990s-2000s. See for example: Khanin, "Vysshee obrazovanie;" Kirill Kobrin, *Gipotezy istorii* (Moscow: Pragmatika kul'tury, 2000), 107-108.
37 A. Savel'ev, *Reformy vysshego obrazovaniya i ih effektivnost'* (Moscow: NIIVO, 2003), 212.
38 See: T. Alikulova, Zh. Barkalova, N. Borodina et al., *Obrazovaniye v Rossii* (Moscow: Moscow State University of Instrument Engineering and Computer Science, 2008), 363.
39 Minobrnauki," RBK.

Several key factors contributed to this tremendous growth. First, the sector of private higher education, which was non-existent in the Soviet period, appeared in 1990 and started to increase very dynamically: while in 1994 the number of private university students was 111 thousand it reached 1.27 million by 2012[40].

Second, there was a tremendous growth in the number of students enrolled in economic, legal, and other social science specialities[41] that under the conditions of post-socialism transition and market reforms were often considered to be more prestigious and promising than those technical specialities that were prioritised in the Soviet period. The quality of teaching in social sciences was rather low during the existence of the USSR, as social sciences were particularly affected by ideological totalitarianism, but even in comparison to this, in the 1990s-2000s the average quality of teaching for the skyrocketing number of students studying economics, law, and some other kinds of social sciences decreased dramatically: the teaching process was not supported by an adequate number of well-qualified and properly selected academic staff[42].

Thirdly, the sharp increase in university admissions was a response to an economic crisis that caused severe cuts in governmental funding. On the one hand, universities proved to be successful in attracting students who paid for their studies and, on the other hand, state universities proved to be efficient lobbyists that managed to obtain the consent of the MES and other higher authorities for opening numerous new specialties not much demanded by the labour market. Actually, the bulk of graduates of these specialities later found themselves unemployed and finally joined the ranks of clerks and shop assistants. On the other hand, as Leibovich and Shushkova argue, the massivisation of the 1990s and 2000s can be considered to be the result of the

---

40   Ibid.
41   The number of students enrolled in technical specialties and especially in natural sciences also grew at that time, but by much smaller rates. See the corresponding diagram in: V. Zvonnikov, *Vysshee professional'noe obrazovanie v oblasti menedzhmenta: statistika razvitia I dinamika izmeneniy (analiticheskiy obzor)* (Moscow: State University of Management, 2009), 19.
42   Khanin, "Vysshee obrazovanie."

pressure from socially active groups of the Russian population[43]. Indeed, the increased demand could seriously support the lobbying efforts of those universities that tried to obtain the approval of higher authorities for opening new specialties and programmes.

The post-Soviet massivisation caused a range of disastrous consequences for Russian higher education. The process provoked a massive influx of weak students, many of whom were just interested in obtaining diplomas by any means, including cheating, bribing teachers, and utilising connections; many other students, attempting to support themselves, tried to combine working with studying and did not attended the majority of classes. At the same time, the rate of growth in the number of students was almost two times higher than the rate of growth in the number of university teachers, thus the academic workload has risen sharply[44]. It prompted many teachers to prepare some lectures hastily: by copying texts from various sources, including available low-quality online texts (such as essays written by students). The quality of control over the educatory process also collapsed, as teachers now did not have sufficient time and strength to identify plagiarism in all the written work to be checked or to prevent all cases of cheating in overcrowded auditoriums during exams. Under these conditions, the actual exam pass criteria have been essentially lowered. In addition, teachers were pressurised by university top managers to turn a blind eye to cheating, as these managers still had to report to the MES average scores of student performance, were not interested in looking bad in such reports, and especially in that per capita funding of their universities would be seriously decreased if many students were dismissed.

As since 2009 the number of students in Russia has started to decline because of an unfavourable demographic situation, and as the country's financial potential has seriously diminished after the global economic crisis of 2007-2009, the Russian government has decided to "optimise" the higher education sector by reducing the number of universities and funded education

---

43 Leibovich and Shushkova, "Na semi vetrah."
44 Calculated by: Alikulova, Barkalova, Borodina et al., *Obrazovaniye*; *Federal'nyi obrazovatel'nyi portal*, http://ecsocman.hse.ru/data/025/643/1219/tablitsa_1_chast.pdf (as of 27 December 2013); Savel'yev, *Reformy*, 212.

programs. In December 2012 the government adopted a road map for "increasing efficiency of science and education," in which it was assumed that during the period between 2012 and 2018 the number of university students should be reduced from 6.5 to 5.1 million while the number of students per university teacher should increase from 9.4 to 12[45]. As some experts argue, this could mean that the number of university teachers will be reduced by 38% during the same period[46]. If such a plan remains largely unchanged, it would mean that the number of university teachers would decrease more rapidly than the number of students and that the already excessive academic workloads would increase again. There is also a serious danger of that large-scale cuts in the number of universities, programmes, and teachers could to a greater extent target those who fight corruption and fraud to ensure the best quality education and research than those who are more successful in financial terms and have more connections and lobbying abilities than other similar actors.

Commercialisation

Unlike massivisation, the *process of commercialisation* has revealed itself only in the post-Soviet period after the socialist system, denying private property, and most of the commercial relations collapsed, and then universities were allowed to charge tuition fees. Already in 1994 there were 111 thousand students in private universities, and by 2001 their number reached 630 thousand[47] and by 2008 it was 1.29 million[48]. It is important to note that during the following years of demographic decline, the number of private university stu-

---

45 "Ob utverzhdenii plana meropriyatii ("dorozhnoi karty") Action Plan "Izmenenia v otrasliah sotsial'noi sfery, napravlennye na povyshenie effektivnosti obrazovania i nauki," *Pravitel'stvo Rossiiskoi Federatsii*, 5 January 2013, http://government.ru/media/files/41d46dc386660b1cccf2.pdf (as of 13 January 2014).

46 Ivan Kurilla, "Eto dazhe ne detsimatsia," *LiveJournal* (15 January 2013), http://alliruk.li vejournal.com/591399.html (as of 28 December 2013).

47 Savel'ev, *Reformy*, 212.

48 Calculated by: "Krizis sokratil negosudarstvennyi sektor v sisteme obrazovania Rossii," http://www.faito.ru/news/1266141284/ (as of 28 December 2013).

dents reduced insignificantly (to 1.27 million by 2012[49]). The education in state higher education institutions is also increasingly commercialised and, as a result, since 2002 the number of students who paid for their studies exceeded the number who did not pay[50].

As students paying for their education has become an increasingly important source of income for universities in comparison to governmental funding, universities have become less and less interested in dismissing even the most poorly performing students of this kind. Superiors rebuke "too principled" teachers by arguing that the latter risks depriving themselves of salaries if the income from fee paying students is reduced. Under such conditions the best that such a principled teacher can do is to make a poorly performing student resit an exam again and again without obtaining a reward for her or his additional work. As fee paying students are usually aware of the fact that they can be dismissed only in extraordinary circumstances, they do not make much effort to improve their knowledge cardinally. Thus, re-examination typically turns into a rite where a teacher seeks a plausible pretext for assigning a passing grade to the student. The situation in many, if not most, private universities is even worse as they have actually turned into "diploma mills", readily issuing diplomas even to those who do not attend classes (sometimes even examinations as well) at all.

Only a handful of the most authoritative state and private Russian universities, predominantly situated in Moscow and St Petersburg, have managed to some extent to resist such a "dictate of commercialisation," as their paid programs are very popular among potential students and thus such universities can allow themselves to dismiss some poorly performing students. It should also be noted that commercialisation affects much more social and some humanitarian programs than physical, mathematical, technology, and other programmes, as in the case with "non-humanitarian" programmes it is much more difficult to obtain a degree without gaining essentially new knowledge in comparison to the knowledge obtained in a secondary school.

---

49 "Krizis sokratil negosudarstvennyi sektor v sisteme obrazovania Rossii," http://www.fai to.ru/news/1266141284/ (as of 28 December 2013).
49 Minobrnauki," RBK.
50 Zvonnikov, *Vysshee*, 9.

Bureaucratisation

Of course, bureaucratisation is not some new phenomenon unknown in the Soviet period. However, its modern wave, which has emerged in the 2000s, looks the strongest. This wave was created, on the one hand, by the federal agencies' aspiration to control the quality of education better and to fight university-level malpractice and, on the other hand, by the development of computer technologies and the Internet that facilitated the writing, modification, and publishing of reports and information online. As a result, universities have been required to be ready for numerous checks by higher authorities, to write an increasing number of voluminous reports and sophisticated syllabi according to detailed and sporadically changing standards, etc. During the most recent "demassivisation" period universities have also had to collect and process a large volume of statistical and other information when trying to comply with "efficiency criteria" introduced by the MES to close or "optimise" (that actually means to cut funding someway) universities found to be "inefficient." Top university managers responded to this "bureaucratisation wave" both by enlarging their bureaucracies at the expense of academic staff[51] and by loading (without paying any additional remuneration) subordinate academics with collecting additional information and writing more reports[52].

The recent wave of bureaucratisation, combined with the "optimisation" campaign has by no means been counterbalanced by the accountability of superiors towards the academic community. On the contrary, it increased discretional powers (e.g. the power of evaluating reports, of determining "efficiency," and, last but not least, of "optimising" or cutting universities, departments, and individual positions) of federal officials towards university management and of the latter towards ordinary academics. The latter have become more vulnerable to informal pressure from superiors, more overloaded, and less capable of controlling students' performance scrupulously. Overall, bureaucratisation while reducing room for some corruption and other fraudu-

---

51 See: Bliakher, "O vnutrennei biurokratii."
52 See for example: Kurilla, "Kriterii otsenki."

lent practices (e.g. for financial machinations by university management) has at the same time created fertile ground for other malpractices.

Growing authoritarianism and reducing autonomy in the higher education system

This process is closely, though in some cases ambiguously, connected with bureaucratisation. The governance system that was established in the majority of Russian universities in the 2000s can be metaphorically described as neo- or quasi-feudal. Rectors have managed to seize nearly absolutist power within many universities (especially in relatively small ones[53]) while university councils and elected assemblies resemble not contemporary parliaments but weak medieval estate assemblies. Specifically, rectors have a wide range of opportunities to influence both such councils' and assemblies' personal compositions (as these bodies include heads of various departments and also other managers) and initiate changes in the principles of these bodies' formation (e.g. increasing the proportion of delegates from administrative personnel at the expense of academic delegates) to ensure the loyalty of the majority of voters[54]. University trade unions are usually even less autonomous and influential, being effectively no more than administrative units subjected to top university management and reluctant to defend the rights of employees during their serious conflicts with university leadership.

The quasi-feudal university management can manifest itself in various ways: in arrogant and disrespectful treatment of subordinates, in using luxury attributes at the workplace, in pressurising members of staff to obey informal orders of the leadership such as to give exceedingly high marks to well-connected students, to turn a blind eye to plagiarism found in unscrupulous

---

[53] As Mikhail Sokolov argues, the power of rectors is stronger in small universities and noticeably weaker in very large universities. See: Mikhail Sokolov, "Rossiiskii universitet kak politicheskaia sistema," *Polit.ru* (29 March 2014), http://polit.ru/article/2014/0 3/29/university/ (as of 5 April 2014).

[54] See: Serghei Golunov, "Kvazifeodalizm vysshego obrazovania," *Troitskiy variant* 123 (2013), http://trv-science.ru/2013/02/26/kvazifeodalizm-vysshego-obrazovaniya (as of 2 February 2014).

students' graduate works, or to work extra time without recompense. The current trend of position and funding cuts in the Russian higher education system makes the rectors' power to decide which professors, departments, and programmes should be cut or allowed to exist even stronger and arbitrary than earlier. The huge and non-transparent powers of rectors inside universities opens a space for the numerous malpractices described in the next part to be performed.

The huge difference between the salaries of university principals and ordinary academics is also one of the main features of "quasi-feudal" relations within universities. While the salaries of ordinary teachers in most Russian universities are comparable to the salaries of shop assistants in the same regions, rectors' salaries, taken together with various bonuses, are typically several dozen times (sometimes even up to more than one hundred times[55]) higher than the typical salaries of docents in the same universities. According to the data from the MES published in June 2013, after the vast majority of rectors ignored the Ministry's order to place such information on their respective universities' sites, the median annual income (before 13% taxation) among the 300 or so rectors included in the list was approximately equivalent 90,000 Euros, while several rectors earned more than 300,000 Euros per a year[56].

While enjoying vast power inside their universities, rectors are rather vulnerable in their relations with the MES and other higher authorities. On the one hand, a rector who has good informal relations with her or his superiors

---

55 For instance, in 2009 the difference between the income of Nizhny Novgorod State University rector and the typical incomes of the same university's dotsents was approximately 100 times. See: For instance, in 2009 the difference between the income of Nizhny Novgorod State University rector and typical incomes of the same university's dotsents was approximately 100 times. See: Sergei Golunov, "Printsy i nishchie ili rossii'skiy vuz kak bananovaya respublika v miniatiure," *Troitskiy variant* 77 (2011), http://trv-science.ru/2011/04/26/princy-i-nishhie-ili-rossijskij-vuz-kak-bananovaya-respublika-v-miniatyure (as of 2 February 2014).

56 "Svedenia o dokhodakh, ob imushchestve i obiazatel'stvah imushchestvennogo haraktera rukovoditelei podvedomstvennyh Minobrnauki Rossii vysshih uchebnyh zavedeniy, a takzhe chlenov ih semei za otchëtnyi finansovyi god s 1 ianvaria 2012 goda po 31 dekabria 2012 goda," *The Ministry of Science and Education of the Russian Federation*, http://goo.gl/DWjf6p (as of 2 February 2014).

can be easily protected from any real competition during the rector's elections, in cases when such elections are held. The mentioned higher authorities are entitled to reject any candidate running for a rector's position without explaining the reasons for the rejection. Since 2006, allegedly to prevent "random people" from taking up the posts of rectors, candidatures for this position should be preliminary approved by special attestation commissions, consisting of representatives of the MES and of various other federal and regional bodies of power and of civic organisations[57]. It means in practice that a qualified candidate usually should have connections in the MES as well as other central and also regional government agencies. In many, if not in the clear majority, of cases only one or two puppet candidates are allowed to compete with a serving rector or a favourite of the higher authorities to make elections formally valid[58]. On the contrary, there were many cases when even those really independent candidates (usually alternative to well-connected favourites or oppositional to the current Russian political regime) who met any formal requirements were disqualified by attestation commissions without any proper explanation of the reasons for the decisions.

On the other hand, rectors can easily be dismissed by higher authorities under various pretexts: violation of some rules and norms, managerial inefficiency or, finally, a standard five-year work contract between a rector and her or his employer can simply not be prolonged upon its expiration. It should be noted that the MES pursues its rectors' rotation policy rather actively: according to my calculation, more than two thirds of the current rectors (or acting rectors) of state universities were appointed no later than in 2005, approximately 40% no later than in 2009, and approximately 25% no later than in 2011[59].

---

57 Federal'nyi zakon o vysshem i poslevuzovskom obrazovanii, 26 August 2006, no 125-F3, article 12.3, http://www.rg.ru/1996/08/29/vysshee-obrazovanie-dok.html (as of 3 February 2014).
58 No wonder that those "puppet candidates", who were asked to run for elections by 'the most probable winners' themselves, are sometimes reluctant to spend their time writing meaningful election programs. I know several cases where such "programs" were simply plagiarised from other sources.
59 The information was calculated by the author after examining Russian universities' official websites.

While rectors are heavily dependent on MES and some other higher authorities, the former are simultaneously considered their most important partners in dialogue on reforming the higher education system. Rectors and their deputies participate in numerous meetings organised by MES and there are a lot of associations of rectors, the umbrella organisation for which is the Union of Russian Rectors, established in 1992 and headed by the rector of MSU Viktor Sadovnichii. In this light, the voices of rectors and their deputies are typically represented as the voices of their university communities, though the interests of ordinary university teachers, who receive tiny salaries and would like to be protected from illegitimate pressure by their bosses, are still hardly heard.

Marginalisation of ordinary university teachers' position

As Shushkova and Leibovich argue, in the post-Soviet period the majority of academics experienced two socio-cultural shocks: in the 1990s they turned from highly-qualified and well-paid specialists to low-paid workers, comparable by their salaries with cleaners, shop assistants, or other low-qualified workers. In the second half of the 2000s, in the course of the bureaucratisation process, academics were also made clerks, who were obliged to report all of their education activities and were evaluated primarily by the quality of numerous reports they have to submit. These shocks, according to Shushkova and Leibovich, were disastrous for Russian academic culture, making it more tolerant to various deviations, including corruption. In particular, moving university teachers into the category of the "new poor" led to the prevalence of vulgar material interests, lowering criteria of estimating one owns actions, and distinguishing between acceptable and inacceptable means of earning, etc.[60]

To be more precise, it can be argued that the typical perceived social status of a post-Soviet Russian university teacher has somewhat schizophrenic features: on the one hand, it still contains the aura of intellectuality

---

60 Shushkova and Leibovich, " 'Hochesh' sdat' ekzamen na piat'?...'."

and prestige, but, on the one hand, it is increasingly perceived as a position of a social looser, who (typically having such visible poverty attributes as old clothes and the absence of a personal car) hardly can be regarded as an example of a success story by her or his students. Adequate information about average university teachers' salaries is not easily available for the public, as top university managers often use various tricks to inflate the figures of salaries in their reports: to report the mean value between very high salaries of the top university managers and the tiny salaries of ordinary teachers, to report salaries just for a single month when all possible yearly bonuses are paid, as if it were the average academic salary, or to report salaries before 13% income is deduced from them, etc. My personal experience (as well as similar experiences of many of my colleagues) of working in an average provincial university shows that a typical net salary of a dotsent having a C.Sc. degree is less than 300 Euros per month, which is compatible with the typical salary of a shop assistant in the same region. A professor of such a provincial university having a D.Sc. degree can likely earn more: around 450-500 Euros.

Anyway, even if official statistics are taken as a basis, one can find that the average salaries of Russian academics are strikingly low in worldwide comparison. According to a joint study by U.S. and Russian researchers, by 2012 Russia was ranked as the second to last in this index among 28 countries considered, being ahead of Armenia only, but behind China, Ethiopia, Kazakhstan, Colombia, Nigeria, and other countries[61]. No wonder that a prominent Slovenian philosopher Slavoj Žižek called Russian university teachers "de facto already part of the proletariat" as they are "ridiculously underpaid."[62] Thus, the low socio-economic status of a teacher is a peculiar feature of the Russian higher education system, though the same problem is also typical for some other post-Soviet countries, such as Ukraine or Armenia.

Miserable salaries together with a poor ability to withstand informal administrative pressure put teachers in a difficult position in terms of motivation.

---

61 Scott Jaschik, "Faculty Pay, Around the World," *Inside High Ed,* 22 March 2012, http://www.insidehighered.com/news/2012/03/22/new-study-analyzes-how-faculty-pay-compares-worldwide (as of 21 February 2014).

62 Slavoj Žižek, "The Revolt of the Salaried Bourgeoisie," *London Review of Books* 34:2 (26 January 2012), http://www.lrb.co.uk/v34/n02/slavoj-zizek/the-revolt-of-the-salaried-bourgeoisie/ (as of 21 February 2014).

It is difficult for them to be either materialists (as salaries are low) or idealists (as they are betweenwhiles pressurised by superiors to give undeservedly good marks to well-connected students).

It should be noted that it is not so easy for a provincial university teacher to change her or his job. The level of academic mobility in Russia is very low: there are almost no true competitions for university teachers' positions (the vast majority of announced competitions are formal and their results are predetermined) and because it is very difficult for a moving teacher to settle away from home on the tiny salary that they obtain. It is also not so easy for a provincial teacher to abandon a university for a position in some other sphere: while in the Russian province it is difficult to find a better job that would more or less suit the qualifications that university teachers usually have, and such teachers would not like to abandon their still formally respectable positions for the available low-skilled jobs even if they are paid better. Still, many teachers have left universities in the post-Soviet period when their conditions of work deteriorated dramatically.

While there are still "silent heroes," who are mostly able to resist pressure while being satisfied with a little, many others choose to leave the system, to take bribes, or to become conformists, considering a wide range of malpractices as something almost normal. This, returning to Leibovich and Shushkova's argument, makes clear why the marginalisation of university teachers' social status leads not only to increasing corruption but also to normalisation of malpractice in the eyes of the academic community.

2.3. Influence of environment

Of course, not all of the factors that create favourable conditions for corruption and cheating are caused just by internal problems of the Russian higher education system. This system exists and developed in a highly aggressive environment that puts a very strong pressure on it. I will consider the social, political, economic, and informational dimensions of this pressure that corrupts the system alongside the afore-mentioned internal processes.

First, universities, and in some cases the MES, are highly vulnerable to the corruption and coercion pressure of powerful political actors: the regime as a whole, top federal and regional politicians, high-standing representatives of law enforcement and security agencies, and other agencies that could paralyse a university's work (e.g. fire or sanitary inspections).

As far as the ruling authoritarian regime is concerned, students form a significant (approximately 6%) but also unreliable part of the Russian electorate, and due to many polling stations being situated in universities themselves or in their dormitories, the regime in some cases is interested in mobilising students for participation in pro-governmental actions, discouraging them from participation in anti-governmental actions, and obtaining a high percent of pro-governmental votes by means of both pro-governmental agitation in universities[63] and various falsifications during the voting process in polling stations controlled by universities. Those universities that might dare to support the opposition or independent civic initiatives for election control could be punished. In the beginning of 2008, after receiving the EU's grant for monitoring Russian elections, the European University in St Petersburg (one of the leading private universities in Russia) was closed for several weeks as the fire inspection found violations of fire safety requirements. Only after the conflict was settled by informal negotiations was the university re-opened[64].

Influential politicians, representatives of law enforcement, security, and other agencies may be interested in ensuring that their children or other relatives get good marks irrespectively of their real performance or in obtaining second (in some cases third) higher education and C.Sc. or D.Sc. degrees for themselves. Rectors, their deputies, heads of departments, other university officials, and ordinary teachers often have good incentives to cooperate with

---

63 See for example: (2012) "V transportnyh vuzah agitiruiut za Putina," *Demagogy.ru*, 21 February 2012, http://demagogy.ru/news/2012-02-21/v-transportnykh-vuzakh-agitiruy ut-za-putina (as of 25 February 2014); "Studenty MFTI zhaluiutsia na davlenie: iesli 'Yedinaya Rossiya' naberët malo golosov, ne dostroyat obschezhitie," *Gazeta.ru*, 24 November 2011, http://www.gazeta.ru/news/lenta/2011/11/24/n_2108970.shtml (as of 25 February 2014).

64 See for example: Anna Pushkarskaia, "Ievropeiskiy universitet vozobnovil rabotu," *Kommersant.ru*, 25 March 2008, http://www.kommersant.ru/doc/870909 (as of 25 February 2013).

influential people in fulfilling such wishes as it can provide informal financial remuneration for them personally as well as other various benefits for them or for their universities or departments. While, it may be risky to stand in the way of such people as they can obtain revenge by various ways: fire, sanitary, and other nit-picking inspections or the personal prosecution of "too principled" teachers, etc. Even the MES can prove to be powerless against top-level officials and politicians. A glaring example of this is a scandalous story about a prominent official from an extremely influential Russian law enforcement agency, whose second higher education diploma (in law) was obtained under questionable circumstances in a dubiously reputed university and it was cancelled by *Rosobrnadzor* after a check conducted in November 2011[65]. However, in January 2012 *Rosobrnadzor* suddenly reversed its decision and again recognised this diploma as legitimate[66].

Rectors may feel themselves vulnerable in such an aggressive environment, not least as a rector's post, which promises a wide range of opportunities to get great formal and informal income, is potentially very attractive for those retired influential officials who obtained their academic degrees by fraudulent ways (this phenomenon will be examined in the next part). Thus, one of the main tasks of university principals is often establishing good relations with regional and, if possible, federal political figures and bodies. No wonder that many rectors willingly go into regional and sometimes federal politics. On the one hand, it gives them a chance to increase their personal status and opens a room for parallel or future political careers. For candidates for the rector's position, membership in the dominant pro-government party United Russia increases the chances of being informally promoted and not being rejected by attestation commissions. On the other hand, United Russia readily includes rectors of state universities in collegial supreme bodies, as it gives the party a more "intellectual" image: noticeably, seven rectors are cur-

---

65 According to a State Duma deputy Aleksandr Khinshtein, the inspection revealed that this official was initially enrolled directly in the fourth year of a university programme and even managed to pass 17 exams within one day. See: Aleksandr Khinshtein, "Nezachiot generala Markina," *Aleksandr Khinshtein*, http://hinshtein.ru/944 (as of 25 February 2014).
66 "Diplom Markina priznan legitimnym," *Stringer,* 11 January 2012, http://www.stringer.ru/Publication.mhtml?Part=37&PubID=19347 (as of 25 February 2014).

rently members of United Russia's Supreme Council. On the whole, among those rectors of state universities who have a right to be members of political parties, at least 39%, according to my calculation (as of July 2013), were members of United Russia while only 1% (six rectors) were members of Just Russia and the Communist Party of Russian Federation, Agrarian Party, and Patriots of Russia were represented only by one rector each. As rectors of private universities (that usually provide an education of lower quality than state universities) generally could not contribute much to improving the intellectual image of the ruling party, it is no wonder that the share of prominent members of United Russia among them is much smaller: according to my imprecise estimation it is likely not more than 10%.

Apart from this, growing authoritarianism also affects negatively the Russian higher educational system in the following way. For many academics, international cooperation and foreign grants are the key opportunities to get additional income and to increase one's own informal status and self-estimation. It also provides a good (though not always working) impetus to adhere to academic integrity standards and not to be involved in malpractice. However, since the second half of the 2000s the regime's policy towards foreign grants, and in some cases towards international cooperation has become more alarmist: foreign grant holders have been increasingly regarded as accomplices of spies or those who would like to discredit Russia. Thus, opportunities for most universities' teaching staff to get additional income via grants has significantly decreased since many popular foreign programmes (such as the George Soros Foundation) were forced to close their offices in Russia. Formally, international funding was largely replaced by funding from Russian sources, but it targets institutions more than individuals and is distributed non-transparently. Indeed, as it will be argued in the next part, the results of major nationwide institutional grant competitions are oftentimes deemed to be greatly influenced by shadow connections and kickback deals.

Apart from the informal pressure and corruptive influence of an authoritarian political system and its powerful representatives, the problem is also in a high tolerance of corruption in Russian society. It is revealing that Russia was ranked 124th-135th in the 2013 Transparency International Corruption

Perception Index[67]. As Leontieva argues, the perception of corruption by the Russian public is ambiguous: on the one hand, bribery among officials is generally condemned but, on the other hand, some forms of low-level corruption as non-monetary rewards for informal services, protectionism, and nepotism, are tolerated by the public[68]. Such tolerance of corruption leads not only to the normalisation of protectionism, gifts, and in some cases even bribes (justified by the low salaries of teachers) in a large part of public opinion but also to widespread readiness to offer bribes to university teachers or to demand them to "help" (e.g. to give an undeservedly high mark or to ask a colleague to do so) those students who are relatives or children of acquaintances.

One more problem is in the widespread attitude towards higher education as something concerning not so much with acquiring special professional knowledge or development of analytical skills but rather just acquiring a diploma by any means to increase one's own social status. Leibovic and Shushkova emphasise that one of the most important types of consumer for the educational services' are the so-called "knights of the times of initial accumulation of capital" (or unscrupulous money-makers of various kinds), who need diplomas just as symbols of high social positions and consider universities as nothing more than shops selling these diplomas[69]. In turn, Orekhovsky stresses the negative role of many employers, which oftentimes also do not need knowledge but diplomas that just certify the graduates' formal status. He argues that Russian business is dominated not by "classic" companies seeking corporate profit maximisation and personnel efficiency that are highly transparent financially, but "gangs" that are indifferent to the quality of the education (as well as to moral values) that the employed staff has, inasmuch as loyalty is estimated by such "gangs" to be a much higher quality than qualifications[70]. However, the influence of the indifference of the "knights of the times of initial accumulation of capital" or "gang-style companies" to the pro-

---

67 *Transparency International*, http://cpi.transparency.org/cpi2013/results/ (as of 26 February 2014).
68 Leontieva, *Institutsionalizatsia*, 21, 98-99.
69 Leibovich and Shushkova, "Na semi vetrah," 147.
70 Orekhovskiy, "Teoria neiavnogo kontrakta."

fessional qualifications of their employers should not be exaggerated: the former hardly constitute the majority of Russian students while the latter is not necessarily the prevailing type of Russian employers, as many positions require high and specialised professional skills anyway.

Finally, Russian higher education faces a challenge from the IT environment that favours plagiarism and examination fraud. Indeed, a large share of the term and graduation papers and even of doctoral theses is copied and pasted from the Internet, while mobile phones and especially smartphones make it easy to receive illegal assistance or to find answers on the Internet during exams. It is now also easy to make small cribs even without careful reading and without handwriting or typing crib texts, which was almost inevitable for crib-makers in the 1990s or earlier. As it will be argued in the fourth part of the book, the responsive reaction by the MES and universities to this challenge is rather weak: plagiarism detection programs and services, mobile communication suppression systems, and other means are used rarely and sporadically. Thus, those who resort to IT for cheating usually have a wider range of opportunities than those who try to prevent it.

2.4. Conclusion

A number of factors, both internal and external to the Russian higher education system, create favourable ground for corruption and cheating. Massivisation, which increased the number of students almost threefold in the 1990s-2000s, has led to an influx of weak students, dramatic lowering of standards of evaluating students' performance, and greatly diminished the teachers' capability to control this performance. Commercialisation has made universities heavily dependent on students' money and reluctant to expel even extremely poorly performing students. Bureaucratisation (coupled with growing authoritarianism and decreasing academic autonomy within the higher education system), though increased financial and teaching restrictions to some extent overloaded ordinary teachers (thus weakening their capability to control students' performance) and broadened the arbitrary power of officials and superiors over their inferiors, thus creating a wide range of opportunities for power abuse. Marginalisation of university teachers' social status has made these teachers poor and tolerant to corruption and undermined their moral authority among students.

As for external influences upon the Russian education system, political authoritarianism has made the MES and universities highly vulnerable to informal pressure and influence from politicians and officials, while public tolerance of low-level and non-monetary forms of corruption makes many people ready to offer bribes to university teachers or to pressure them into rendering protection to some students not happy with their marks. Both among entrants or students and among employers of graduates there is a widespread attitude towards higher education as just to obtain diplomas by any means regardless of real knowledge and skills that are theoretically certified by such diplomas. Finally, the changing IT environment makes technologies easily available for those students and scholars who resort to cheating while the MES and universities do not have sufficient will or resources to stop it.

Of course, the overall picture is more complicated: probably a much wider range of factors favour corruption and cheating while some other factors (e.g. official and activists' anti-corruption and anti-cheating efforts—to be discussed in the fourth part) hinder it. However, the examined trends are especially powerful and pervasive and one can hardly expect that they could be reversed in the foreseeable future.

3 CORRUPTION AND CHEATING PRACTICES

As shown in the previous chapter, there are a lot of vulnerabilities in the Russian higher education system and a lot of opportunities to exploit these vulnerabilities for fraudulent purposes. Similarly, there are a wide range of corruption or cheating practices used by unscrupulous managers, academics, support staff, or students. As in the majority of other countries, Russian higher education malpractices do not have any significant national peculiarities: indeed, their perpetrators use largely the same stratagems exploiting the same system weaknesses to give or accept bribes and kickbacks, embezzle institutional funds, plagiarise, cheat during examinations, and shelter protégés, etc.

This part focuses on analysing such malpractices, which are largely divided into two major groups: corruption and cheating. In the first section of this part I consider the relevant conceptual issues including definitions and classifications. Then in the next two sections I examine how the two mentioned groups of malpractices—corruption and cheating—are employed by unscrupulous perpetrators. Finally, the effects of such malpractices on Russian higher education and on Russian society will be considered.

3.1. Conceptualisations

Malpractice in education is studied from the viewpoints of many disciplines: economics, sociology, law, and political science. A large part of such research is done by policy analysts supported by international organisations. Such studies try to categorise malpractice, establish reasons for its pervasiveness, develop adequate methods for investigating it, and, finally, find efficient recipes for solving these problems.

As stated in the introduction, corruption is typically understood to be an abuse of power for private gain[71]. Some authors add more features to this formula, such as the systematic character of such abuse and the considerable extent of its influence over the access and quality of education[72]. On the other hand, the term "corruption" is sometimes used as an equivalent of almost any malpractice or form of academic misconduct (including academic cheating): specifically any behaviour that is aimed at obtaining any improper benefits either for this person or for somebody else even without an abuse of power[73].

Emphasising the term "corruption" as the key concept of research on education-related malpractices can create several conceptual problems.

First, both "wide" and "narrow" definitions create their own specific problems. If a definition is too wide, it could be difficult to denote clearly the phenomenon to be fought in practice and the specific measures required. If a definition is too narrow, there is a risk of not conceptualising some relevant malpractices that do not meet some specific criteria, e.g. if malpractices are not systematic, if they do not significantly influence the access or quality of higher education, etc.

Second, the borders of corruption are unclear. There is a large 'grey zone' between corruption and unethical or ethically ambiguous behaviour[74]. The fact that a university teacher is engaged in tutoring students from the same university can be considered as normal, ethically controversial, or as an act of corruption, depending on additional circumstances, such as a teacher's capability to influence future evaluation of these students. Similarly, some questionable cases of using institutional resources for private purposes by a university employee (small-scale printing and copying, collecting airline and hotel bonus points, or not paying for a spouse brought on a business trip and staying in the same hotel room, etc.) can be considered as normal, minor violation, or as serious misconduct depending on the scale of such use and of a specific organisation's policy concerning such practices. Some particular

---

71 See, for example: Hallak and Poisson, *Corrupt Schools*, 29.
72 Ibidem.
73 Leontieva, *Institutsionalizatsia*, 93.
74 Hallak and Poisson, *Corrupt Schools*, 32.

practices, such as small gifts to teachers or even treating them after graduation exams or theses defences (as is often the case in Russia) can be considered as generally acceptable in countries belonging to some cultural traditions but quite unacceptable in countries belonging to other cultural traditions. In some cases unacceptable actions (falsification of reports or over-marking students, etc.) may be caused either by a perpetrator's wish to defend corporative interests (e.g. to prevent closure of an institution or job cuts) or her or his incompetence with no monetary motives involved[75].

The border between corruption and cheating, which is especially important in the light of the current study, is also not always clear. As Sajó argues, while corruption means that "several parts may benefit" cheating implies that "only the malefactor benefits."[76] However, there can be cases related to extortion (that is a sort of corruption) when all sides except a bribe-taker lose rather than win; apart from this, widespread exam cheating can be beneficial for university teachers and managers as it can improve indices of reports on students' performance and release not too principled teachers from re-examining poorly performing students. Alternatively, it can be argued that cheating implies such cases where perpetrators not so much abuse their powers as try to hide their malpractices from those who supervise the legal order. This approach however, would also be vulnerable to criticism, as those who abuse their powers often try to hide their misdeeds from supervising authorities, while many of those who resort to cheating (e.g. high-standing officials defending doctoral theses written by somebody else) abuse their powers. While it is often difficult to draw a strict line to distinguish between real cases of corruption and cheating, using both pairs of characteristics ("one part benefits" vs "several parts benefit" and "abuse of power" vs "hiding from a superior") may be helpful to some extent for a rough delimitation between the two domains.

---

75 Chapman, *Corruption*, 3-5.
76 András Sajó, "Academic Malpractice. European Higher Education at Risk," in Hossam Badravi et al., eds *The management of university integrity: proceedings of the seminar of the Magna Charta Observatory 19 September 2007* (Bologna: Bononia University Press, 2008).

Third, it should be taken into account that corruption or cheating cannot be legally punished in all cases, even if an offence can be interpreted as a veiled form of bribe-taking. Sometimes a violation of an ethical code is the only valid ground for a malefactor's punishment. Thus, in terms of punishment for corruption and cheating, they can be considered either from legal or from ethical viewpoints, or both.

Higher education malpractice could be classified in various ways. The first possible way is dividing such cases of malpractice into two general categories—corruption and cheating—as is used in the current book. Some other, less general categories of specific malpractices (e.g. embezzlement, bribery, fraud, extortion, and favouritism[77]) could be also emphasised. The second way is to emphasise spheres in which malpractices happen. One of the most detailed classifications of this kind[78], offered by Hallak and Poisson, lists ten major educational areas (finance; allocation of specific allowances; construction, maintenance, and repairs; distribution of equipment, furniture, and materials; writing of textbooks; teacher appointment, management, payment, and training; teacher behaviour (professional misconduct); information systems; examinations and diplomas; and institution accreditation) and malpractices relevant to each of these areas[79]. It is also possible to emphasise the levels (ministerial, university, and centres controlling university admission exams) at which corruption practices occur or also the scale (large, medium, or small) of such practice's impacts on the higher education system. Of course, this list of possible classification criteria is not exhaustive.

Being aware of the blurred borders between various educational malpractices and between clearly unacceptable practices and tolerated behaviour, as well as the existence of various options to classify educational malpractices, I do not claim that the conceptual approach used in this part is optimal or this approach's superiority over other possible conceptualisations. At the same time, I have some conceptual preferences. Malpractices are divided into corruption and cheating (that, in their turn, are subdivided into more spe-

---

77 Inge Amundsen, *Corruption. Definition and Concepts* (Bergen: Chr. Michelsen Institute, 2000). Cited by: Hallak and Poisson, *Corrupt Schools*, 57.
78 In these cases all malpractices are considered as corruption in its broad meaning.
79 Hallak and Poisson, *Corrupt Schools*, 62-63.

cific malpractices), which typically, though not necessarily always, differ by the extent of the abuse of power ("pure" cheating does not involve it) and by unilateral (cheating) or multilateral (corruption) beneficiaries from such practices. Though real malpractices can combine features of both corruption and cheating, more pronounced features either of the former or of the latter can usually be prioritised.

As for classifying malpractices, I will try to use the mentioned classifications involving levels, areas of planning, scales, and sorts of malpractices combined and (in the case of planning areas) slightly modified in comparison to classifications offered by other authors. This approach will be applied in the two following sections to corruption and cheating.

3.2. Corruption

Various methods of abusing power for obtaining illicit gain flourish at all levels and in all planning areas of the Russian higher education system. I will consider the following levels of corruption in the higher education system: ministerial level, university level (including the sublevels of university management, ordinary university teachers, and students), university's relations with external actors, and entrance exams (the USE system).

Corruption practices at the top level of the system, viz. at the level of the MES and federal ministries and agencies supervising universities, are largely known from anecdotes, rumours, and speculations rather than from reliable facts that explicitly confirm the widespread suspicions of the Russian academic community towards what is happening at the ministry level. It does not mean that this level has low-corruption as numerous prerequisites for corruption are present, including non-transparency and wide ranging opportunities for abuse of power in such fields as attestation and accreditation of universities, approving new universities' teaching programmes and opening of dissertation councils, appointments of acting rectors, distribution of governmental funding, confirming results of doctoral theses' defences, and composing final lists of winners of olympiads for schoolchildren, etc. The scarcity of available facts, relevant to high-level malpractices in these and other situations can be explained both by high latency of such malpractices and by the anti-corruption control over ministries' activities as being weak.

One of the main potential opportunities for corrupt ministry-level officials is attestation and accreditation of universities, opening programmes, and dissertation councils, etc. Those officials, who are involved in such activities, have large room for arbitrary decisions: they can be either captious or appeaseable while checking various report data. It is a common practice in Russia to lavish care upon controllers: to transport them in good cars, to treat them in restaurants, to arrange city tours, and to gift expensive souvenirs. Of course, not only such relatively modest signs of respect can be offered but also evident bribes. Similarly, university delegations bringing reports or applications to Moscow allegedly often try to obtain support from some promoters, whose help may not always be altruistic.

As was mentioned before, the post of a university rector is very attractive in terms of both official income and of various shadowy opportunities to make profit. Taking into account that appointments of acting rectors and procedures of disqualifying alternative candidates for participating in rectorial elections are highly non-transparent there is a high danger that rector positions in some cases could be distributed for bribes, subsequent kickbacks, rendering some services in return, or due to connections. Similarly, current rectors cannot be sure they will not be removed due to some far-fetched pretext to empty their positions for some well-connected candidates. It is important that instead of a retired principal the MES or some other supervising ministry can appoint an acting rector until elections (that can be delayed for an indefinite time) that often turn out to be formal, as a new head usually has enough time and power to make the election assembly loyal to her or his candidature. Since the 2000s there has been an increasing trend of appointing retired influential officials as rectors despite many such officials (as it will be shown below) having defended their C.Sc. or D.Sc. theses under rather dubious circumstances; this kind of appointment in some cases can be compared to the medieval practice of awarding a vassal an estate for the vassal's previous service.

Some cases of rectors' dismissals or of appointing acting rectors, involving controversial and non-transparent decisions at the ministerial levels, can be mentioned as an alarming sign that corruption in such situations is possible at least potentially. Here are three cases of strange appointments or dismissals, all of which took place in 2013.

In the first case a 34-year-old rector of a private university (whose mother was the head of a regional education ministry[80]) became a favourite candidate for rector elections to be held in a large regional state university. Later this person decided to withdrew his candidacy after some bloggers accused him of dissertation fraud[81]. After this all the other candidates except one also withdrew their candidatures, which made the elections legally invalid, and meant that the MES had to appoint an acting rector who was none other than the same person who had had to withdraw initially,[82] despite the accusation not being convincingly responded to.

In another case, an influential regional politician and businessman (the originality of whose C.Sc. thesis was also put into question by activists[83]) was appointed as an acting rector of a regional state university by the MES after the candidature of this person for a rector's position was rejected by an attestation commission as an invalid candidate who did not meet the necessary qualification requirements[84].

In the third case a rector of an agrarian state university, who was a principal only for three months during 2012, was fired by the Ministry of Agri-

---

80 It is noteworthy that this person graduated from a private university that was headed by his father. The mentioned person was also the executive director of the same university since he was 18. See: See: Aleksandr Fridom, "Media-kholding 'Regiony Rossii': Syn ministra obrazovania Marii El s 'lipovoi dissertatsiei' stal rektorom MarGU," *7x7-journal.ru,* 21 April 2014, http://7x7-journal.ru/post/41050 (as of 6 May 2014).

81 *Obshchestvennyi komitet po bor'be s korruptsiiei v Mari El,* "Syn ministra obrazovania RME i vozmozhnyi rektor MarGU zaschitil 'lipovuiu' dissertatsiiu?!," *LiveJournal,* 15 February 2013, http://no-korrupcia.livejournal.com/15953.html (as of 11 March 2014).

82 "Mariiskii gosuniversitet vozglavil syn respublikanskogo ministra obrazovania," *Lenta.ru,* 18 March 2013, http://lenta.ru/news/2013/03/18/margu/ (as of 11 March 2014).

83 Yurii Bogomolov, "Rektor RGU im. Yesenina g-n Pupkov: doktor – ne doktor, plagiat – ne plagiat," *7x7-journal.ru,* 25 December 2012, http://7x7-journal.ru/post/23802 (as of 11 March 2014).

84 It should also be noted that another three from four candidates for the rector's position were also disqualified (with just one candidate remaining) that made the elections technically invalid. See: "Naznachen ispolniaiushchii obiazannosti rektora Riazanskogo gosuniversiteta," *Mediariazan',* 21 December 2012, http://mediaryazan.ru/news/detail/159918.html (as of 20 February 2014).

culture supposedly for the university's bad performance in 2011 (in the year when this person was not a rector) and was replaced by a high-standing retired official, who had earlier held a prominent official position in the region when it was headed by the current Minister of Agriculture[85].

There is a wide range of potential opportunities for high-level corruption related to the distribution of governmental funding for universities, departments, research groups, and individual academics. The first kind of such opportunities involves lobbying for the opening new educational programmes or university-level research institutions and of funding additional student positions, etc. The second kind can be potentially related to the awarding of competitive funding: grants, government purchase orders, and special statuses to universities (implying additional funding), etc. In particular, as Onishchenko claimed, some government purchasing competitions organised by the MES were actually just the distribution of money among organisations that had shadowy ties with the ministry's officials as personal connections, participation of such organisations' representatives in working groups responsible for determining conditions of competitions[86], or, vice versa, participation of high-standing officials in executive boards of organisations winning such competitions[87]. In some cases, competitions were surprisingly won by suspiciously small and little known organisations whose contact information sometimes was not even available to the public[88].

The integrity of the process of approving C.Sc. and D.Sc. theses by the VAK, designed to be a barrier against awarding degrees for low-quality and falsified dissertations defended in universities, sometimes also raises serious questions. While many theses of high-ranking officials are very suspicious and many such officials (as it will be shown later in this part) were accused of plagiarism or other kinds dissertation fraud, I do not know of any high-profile

---

85 See: "V Chuvasshkoi gosudarstvennoi sel'skohoziaystvennoi akademii vybiraiut rektora," *Natsional'naia teleradiokompania Chuvashii*, (13 June 2013), http://www.nt rk21.ru/video.aspx?id=2788 (as of 30 May 2014).
86 Yevgeniy Onishchenko, "Kormlenie kak sistema."
87 Yevgeniy Onishchenko, "FTsP: konkursy i 'konkursy'."
88 Ivan Sterlingov, "Milliony dollarov komissaram "Nashikh" i firmam bez telefona i ofisa," *Slon.ru*, 25 January 2012, http://slon.ru/future/milliony_dollarov_komissaram_nashikh _i_firmam_bez_telefona_i_ofisa-734475.xhtml (as of 12 March 2014).

cases when a thesis from any high-ranking official (governor, member of parliament, or minister) or from an official working for the MES has been rejected by the VAK. On the contrary, there have been cases when the VAK refused to consider, or declined without providing any reasoned explanations, appeals of academic activists, who requested the revoking of academic degrees of officials or university rectors reasonably suspected of dissertation fraud[89]. Some cases of conflict of interest, when members of expert councils of the VAK were simultaneously members of university-level dissertation councils where suspicious theses were defended, were pointed out by observers[90]. Last but not least, between August 2012 until April 2013 (when the below mentioned person was arrested for a reason not related to his work in the MES) the VAK was headed by Felix Shamkhalov, a person who, without having any extraordinary academic achievements, made a fantastically quick academic carrier, defending his C.Sc. thesis in economics just a year after graduating from a university, and defending his D.Sc. thesis in economics only four years after that, and becoming a corresponding member of the RAS just eight years after his graduation. During the short period of Shamkhalov's office the term of appeals against decisions to award doctoral degrees was diminished from ten to just three years that effectively made it not possible to legally challenge a very large part, if not a majority, of the suspicious theses written by officials in the post-Soviet period.

At the level of universities, corruption practices are more diverse and documented. Unlike cases of top-level corruption, such practices are revealed and punished relatively often. While university managers of different levels have more opportunities for extracting corruption profit than ordinary teachers, bribery is so widespread among the latter that it is very difficult to estimate if managers or ordinary teachers are more corrupt.

Russian university managers benefit from corruption in the majority of the afore-listed education planning areas. Some are involved in financial

---

89 Andrei Rostovtsev, "Duh zakhvatyvaet ot takikh istoriy," *LiveJournal,* 21 June 2013, http://afrikanbo.livejournal.com/322401.html (as of 12 March 2014); Sergei Parkhomenko, "Malen'kie sekretiki bol'shogo ministerskogo doma," *LiveJournal,* 14 November 2013, http://cook.livejournal.com/244412.html (as of 12 March 2014).

90 See for example: Andrei Rostovtsev, "Lipovaia ekonomika. Chast' III," *LiveJournal,* 17 December 2013, http://afrikanbo.livejournal.com/346042.html (as of 12 March 2014).

fraud. Despite governmental financial control over universities having been tightened noticeably since the 2000s, some fraudulent schemes still exist, such as transferring money to front companies for services not actually rendered or misusing money from so-called rector's funds that are formed from extra-budgetary revenues and controlled by supervisors poorly[91].

Some managers receive procurement kickbacks from suppliers of various goods and services for their universities, granting such suppliers a monopoly position and purchasing their goods and services for inflated prices[92]. Others illegally rent out university space to non-affiliated companies[93].

Some organise the open or slightly covert selling of university diplomas for those who actually do not study at all or just fulfil a minimum of necessary formalities. This shadow business is practiced by corrupt managers of some, including prestigious, state universities[94]. As for Russian private universities, it should be noted that a large part, if not a majority of them are essentially a diploma selling business: at least in some of these universities students may not even attend their classes and do not take exams without a risk of being penalised. Sometimes diplomas are sold by shadow partnerships between state and private universities. This kind of scheme involves so-called *vuzy-prokladki* ("laying universities"), which means private universities that are entitled to award graduates diplomas from their partner institutions—larger and more respectable state universities. In practice this scheme can actually imply the selling of diplomas from state universities to those bogus students who received bad marks at the USE and even who do not attend their classes

---

[91] See for example: Bashir Imaev, "Bashkirskiy gosudarstvennyi agrarnyi universitet: slagaemye neeffektivnosti," *Ufa gubernskaia*, 31 December 2012, http://ufagub.net/i ndex.php?option=com_content&view=article&id=33338551:2012-12-31-03-59- 50&Itemid=6 (as of 12.03.2014).

[92] See for example: Andrei Chashkin, "Uborka s otkatom," *Kommersant.ru*, 11 March 2013, http://www.kommersant.ru/doc/2143499 (as of 13 March 2014); Viktor Oref'ev, "Prigovor po delu Pavla Sidorova: srok, shtraf i lisheniye nagrad," *Biznes-klass*, 15 June 2012, http://bclass.ru/novosti/prigovor-po-delu-pavla-sidorova-srok-shtraf-i-lishe nie-nagrad (as of 13 March 2014).

[93] See for example: "Oshtrafovan prorektor MGPU, kotoryi nezakono sdaval pomesh- chenia vuza v arendu," *Infonedvizhka.ru*, 28 April 2011, http://infonedvizhka.ru/accide nt/192/ (as of 7 April 2014).

[94] See for example: Natalia Shiriaeva, "Kupit' diplom: ovchinka vydelki ne stoit," *Real- isty*, http://www.realisti.ru/main/educ?id=173 (as of 19 March 2014).

while studying in these "laying universities." The leadership of both partner universities involved in such schemes (sometimes the same people) are beneficiaries of this fraudulent scheme[95].

Some managers distribute bonuses and grants among themselves or their protégés (in the latter case often for kickbacks in return), collect "tributes" from those successful collectives that obtained funding for their projects (those university administrators who actually do not work in these projects receive payments as if they really worked), force subordinates to mention them as co-authors of research works or inventions, or go to international conferences instead of those scholars who really deserve it.

Some managers protect well-connected students and candidates for post-graduate degrees either for material or non-material profit, place applicants[96] on post-graduate courses for money[97], give jobs to relatives[98] and familiar persons[99], sell queue positions for students claiming accommodation in dormitories, or covertly rent dormitory rooms to strangers[100].

---

95 See for example: Dmitriy Kiselëv, "Vuzy-prokladki: moshenniki nashli sposoby oboiti EGE," *Vesti nedeli*, 22 September 2013, http://vesti7.ru/news?id=41336 (as of 13 March 2013).
96 It should be stressed that for many young male applicants enrolling on a post-graduate course is a very attractive option allowing them to avoid conscription.
97 See for example: Mikhail Falaleev, "Sotrudniki vuza predlagali stat' aspirantom za million," *Rossiiskaia gazeta*, 18 March 2014, http://www.rg.ru/2014/03/18/vzatka-site.html (as of 18 March 2014).
98 The practice of giving senior positions to relatives is very widespread in private universities. In the course of my research, conducted at the beginning of 2013, I identified about 60 private and only two state universities where the governing bodies included two or more relatives. This information is incomplete as I did not cover numerous filial branches of universities, as some close relatives working in universities' governing bodies could be not identified because of different surnames, and also because many private institutions do not publish any information about their governing bodies on their sites.
99 In 2012 I heard from a trustworthy source a story about when a young lady with no academic record and achievements managed to get the job of English language teacher in a large medical state university due to her personal connections in the regional government, who in their turn had personal connections with the rector of that university.
100 "Programma," *Rossiiskii studencheskii soiuz*, http://russiansu.ru/publ/7-1-0-46/

Top managers buy luxury cars at the expense of the universities[101], and use those cars as their own. They also practice so-called "academic tourism," going abroad under the pretext of concluding agreements on cooperation (which afterwards do not actually work) with foreign universities, but actually primarily for personal purposes[102].

Another form of "academic tourism" is visiting conferences at the sending university's expense without having the aim of making a valuable contribution to their work. There are even some signs of businesses promoting "academic tourism" from post-Soviet countries to the EU and other regions of the world at the sending universities' expense. Last year I received some junk e-mail messages from companies advertising strange conferences: one of these junk e-mails advertised conferences held three times a month during the entire year in the Czech Republic, Poland, and Bulgaria. The organisers did their best to attract as many post-Soviet researchers as possible: conference topics (such as "Days of Science" or "Contemporary Academic Achievements," etc.) were made as broad and vague as possible. The main target group for such announcements is probably just those who have power or connections to get funding from their universities for participating in these conferences.

It is very difficult to identify the most widespread practices employed by university managers both because such practices are usually highly latent and because no relevant statistical data on detected cases are available. The

---

101 In 2011-2012 there were several scandals involving those universities that tried to buy prestigious cars at the price of more than €110,000 for their rectors and other top managers. See: 101 In 2011-2012 there were several scandals involving those universities that tried to buy prestigious cars at the price of more than $ 150,000 for their rectors and other top managers. See: "Minobrnauki prokommentirovalo zaiavki vuzov na zakupki dorogikh inomarok," *RIA Novosti*, 1 September 2012, http://ria.ru/society/2 0120901/734933376.html (as of 2 February 2012).

102 I know for sure of one case when a rector of a large state university concluded a co-operation agreement with one university from the Canary Islands during his trip there. After this trip he asked his subordinates to prepare proposals on what this cooperation could be about. Another example was provided to me by the head of a UK university department, who stated that several years ago he and his colleagues were very surprised when their partners from a large Siberian university brought to the UK more than 30 people, who all were "members of a football team," for participation in a friendly football match in the framework of a bilateral cooperation program.

results of analysing 15 cases of rectors' arrests (occurring between 2001 and 2013), which I managed to find via Google.com search, could probably be of some help when identifying the key trends of corruption at the level of university top management. While the most common accusation against rectors of state universities was taking or extorting bribes from suppliers of goods and services, rectors of private universities were most commonly accused of taking or extorting bribes from their students or issuing diplomas to those who actually did not study.

The low-level corruption involving those ordinary teachers and clerks, who have much fewer powers than their managers, is probably less diverse and sophisticated than corruption practices involving high-standing university managers (taking into account that the latter usually can apply the same practices as the former plus some other malpractices based on specific powers they have) but hardly less widespread and deeply rooted. The most widespread form of low-level corruption is probably bribery of unscrupulous teachers by students or other kinds of bribe-givers in exchange for positive marks. It is often difficult to reveal the cases of bribery for several reasons: 1) bribe-takers oftentimes use intermediaries; 2) many poorly performing students are quite happy that this method of solving their problems exists; and 3) the current legislation on bribery and corruption is not generally applicable to university teachers as they are not civil servants[103]. Yet there are many cases when bribe-taking university teachers are convicted and punished[104].

Apart from the direct monetary bribing of teachers by students, there are many other corruption practices at this level. Teachers exploit students' labour or use other services in return for positive marks[105], compel them to

---

103 See: Gennadii Morozov, "Korruptsia v obrazovanii: mify i realii normativno-pravovogo haraktera," *Pedagogicheskoe obrazovanie Rossii* 2 (2010): 149-159.
104 See for example: *Pravo.ru*, "Osuzhdën prepodavatel' iurinstituta FSIN, slishkom vysoko tsenivshii otlichnikov," 19 June 2012, http://pravo.ru/news/view/73826/ (as of 13 March 2014).
105 See for example: "Esli my chego-to ne znali, s nas prosto brali obeshchanie ne rabotat' khirurgami," *Esquire*, 28 April 2011, http://esquire.ru/med-students (as of 13 March 2014).

buy study guides[106] or to pay for private tuition[107], protect some privileged students and discriminate against others, practice sexual harassment[108], or appropriate grant funds[109] etc. Clerks can be involved in stealing money or some corporeal property or selling secret information about exam questions to students. Both teachers and clerks act as intermediaries in bribe-taking, or render a service of "solving problems" to those students who have problems with passing exams or who have importunately asked "too principled" teachers not to be too strict to their "relatives" or "children of very close friends."[110] In some cases such intermediary schemes can be no more than deceiving one of the main parties involved: a bribe-giving student may not suspect that the teacher does not know about the offer[111] while a teacher, disinterestedly agreeing not to be too strict towards her or his colleague's protégé, may not suspect that this colleague receives money for this business or even fraudulently appropriates money supposedly needed for bribing this teacher.

Students can participate in corruption schemes both as voluntary bribe-givers and as victims of extortion, they also participate in bribery as intermediaries, transferring money to corrupt teachers[112]. According to surveys con-

---
106 See for example: "Za vziatku osudili 73-letnego prepodavatelia MarGU," *Downhouse.ru*, 14 June 2011, http://down-house.ru/blog/Sofia/35024-za-vzyatku-osudili-73-letnego-prepodavatelya-margu.html (as of 13 March 2014).
107 See for example: *Juridicheskaya konsul'tatsia onlain*, 24 January 2014, http://www.9 111.ru/questions/q3248595-vzyatka-prepodavatelyu.html#breadcrumbs (as of 13 March 2014).
108 See for example: Ol'ga Zhuravlëva, "Seksual'nye domogatel'stva v vuzakh," 12 September 2010, http://www.echo.msk.ru/programs/tsluchay/708990-echo/ (as of 13 March 2014).
109 There are various ways to do this: to falsify a sociological survey that actually was not held or to pay for other persons' services (translation or transportation, etc.) that actually were not rendered, etc. In many cases it is not very difficult in Russia to obtain a blank receipt or a "second invoice" (stating a different amount in comparison with the real one) from a supplier, which also opens wide opportunities either to appropriate some part of the funding or to spend it for unauthorised purposes.
110 Leontieva, *Institutsionalizatsia*, 230.
111 In such cases a bogus intermediary keeps a bribe if a student gets a good mark and returns the bribe if a student receives a bad mark as if the teacher declined the offer.
112 In many cases intermediary students are very cautious and do not advertise their services to everyone; so it is the task of a potential bribe-giver to identify an intermediary who can really "solve a problem" with a teacher and not to take money for nothing. See: Leontieva, *Institutsionalizatsia*, 278-284.

ducted by various Russian researchers in the 2000s, around 20% of students were involved in bribe-giving[113]. In 2013 researchers from the HSE estimated the share or bribe-givers at 9%, while 17% of respondents were inclined to do it under some circumstances[114]. Some other recent results are, however, less optimistic: for example, according to the results of an online survey, conducted by the Career.ru website, 22% of students admitted that they gave bribes and 42% of them claimed they did it under pressure from university teachers[115].

It is commonly believed that the majority of bribe-givers and victims of extortion among students are those who perform poorly; such students are largely happy with having the opportunity to solve their problems by bribing if the requested amount of money is not too large. Many poorly performing students do not want to deal with a too principled teacher who does not take bribes[116].

As for corrupt relations between actors representing a university and external actors, the majority of such relations (relations between top university managers and suppliers or between powerful officials and pressurised teachers, etc.) have already been described above. It should be noted that in some cases universities indirectly create strong demand for shadow services: "ghost writing" for students and scholars (to be considered in the section "Cheating") or the selling of sickness certificates by doctors of medical centres for those students who wish to qualify for an extended examination period, etc.

Finally, one more level of corruption in the Russian higher education system is related to the Unified State Exam and those olympiads for schoolchildren that give prize-winners the right to enter the relevant university programmes without taking entrance exams.

The USE was introduced as an experiment in 2001 and has become the dominant form of university entrance examination since 2009. In its con-

---

113 See for example: Ibid., 268.
114 E.B. Galitskiy, "O vuzovskoi desiatine, razmere vziatok i prochem," *Akkreditatsia v obrazovanii* 70 (2014): 27.
115 "Kazhdyi piatyi student gotov zaplatit' vziatku v zimniuiu sessiu," *Career.ru*, 29 January 2014, http://career.ru/article/14612?nocookies (as of 7 April 2014).
116 Ibid, 274-276.

ception the USE was designed to provide equal opportunities for provincial students entering prestigious universities and to eliminate corruption at entrance exams. Indeed, before the USE became the dominant form of university entrance examination, such corruption was very widespread. Rectors and their deputies protected well-connected enrolees: there was an almost omnipresent phenomenon of "rectors' lists," consisting of those enrolees who should be given sufficiently high marks by examiners[117]. Secretariat staff organised other schemes combining corruption and fraud, such as the substitution of written works or falsification of entrance exam scores.

Unfortunately, the introduction of the USE did not help to eradicate corruption at entrance exams. Though the illicit influence of top university managers and secretariat workers on determining who is eligible to enter has been weakened considerably, it has not been removed completely. Rectors and vice-rectors still have powers to decide who is eligible to enter if several enrolees who have the same scores are competing for a smaller number of university places. Some fraudulent schemes are still used, as can best be illustrated by the 2011 high profile scandal involving the Pirogov Russian National Research Medical University (one of the leading Russian medical universities). It was discovered that fake enrolees with very high USE scores were included in the list of applicants. Those uninformed enrolees who had slightly lower scores found themselves not passing and withdrew their applications. After this, those fake enrolees were removed from the list (as they withdrew their applications voluntary), emptying places for those informed candidates, who had lower scores than the misled applicants with good scores who were prompted to withdrew. It was estimated that only 20 "real" enrolees had sufficient scores to enter at the first stage of the competition while nearly 800 university places were at stake. Though *Rosobrnadzor* took some measures, aimed at prevent using such tricks again (such as automatic

---

[117] See for example: "Skol'ko stoit v vuz ustroit'. MK v Pitere rasskazyvaet o 'tenevykh sposobakh postuplenia v institut," *Garant*, http://legalru.ru/document.php?id=30006 (as of 14 March 2014).

checking of the lists of entrants with the aim of finding fake data)[118], one can hardly guarantee that some similar (e.g. involving real applicants with very high scores) or other fraudulent schemes are not used or could not be used in the future.

More importantly, the USE just shifted the focus of corruption related to university entrance exams from the level of a university's top management to the level of provincial agencies responsible for education and of ordinary school teachers who maintain the order during exams and check the USE work of secondary school graduates. Regional authorities and directors of schools pressurise ordinary teachers monitoring exams to turn a blind eye to cribbing by peculiar examinees or even to "help" them to answer questions correctly; bribed teachers also do the same things by their own initiative[119]. After an exam the work of a protected examinee can be substituted with that from another, which is again done by a teacher[120]. There are also suspicions that the USE questions are leaked to some students from various levels: provincial education agencies, schools, and even the MES[121].

Some Russian regions have gained a notorious public reputation for the pervasiveness of USE-related corruption practices. First of all, it concerns the republics of the Northern Caucasus, especially Dagestan: numerous poorly performing school graduates from these republics entering prestigious universities with nearly maximal USE scores have become proverbial. There is even a phenomenon of "USE-tourism" when school-leavers from various Russian regions purposefully go to the North Caucasian republics to take ex-

---

118 Dmitrii Kaistro, "Rosobrnadzor pridumal kak ne dopustit' skandala s mërtvymi dushami," *Vesti.ru,* 14 August 2011, http://www.vesti.ru/doc.html?id=537827&tid=92454 (as of 15 March 2014).
119 See for example: Artur Lesnov, "Kak my sdavali EGE," http://scepsis.net/library/id_3023.html (as of 15 March 2013).
120 In some cases officials of provincial education agencies are also involved in such substitution. See for example: "V Astrakhani dvuh chinovnikov podozrevaiut v podmene rezul'tatov EGE," *Interfax.ru,* 31 May 2012, http://www.interfax.ru/russia/248428 (as of 15 March 2014).
121 See for example: "Prichina utechki rezul'tatov EGE – korruptsia v Minobrnauki," *Rossiiskii studencheskii soiuz,* http://russiansu.ru/publ/2-1-0-203 (as of 15 March 2014).

ams, as it is easy to find necessary contacts in such regions and as bribe amounts for passing the USE successfully are not very high[122].

Olympiads for schoolchildren are an alternative way for enrolees either to enter a university without taking the USE exams or to get a 100% score for the exam on an olympiad's subject. Taking a prize in an olympiad held by a specific state university gives the winner a privilege for entering this university only, while taking a prize at an all-Russian olympiad gives the enrolee privileges for entering any relevant programme at any state university. Some state universities give prize-winners of olympiads organised by them a very significant percent (e.g. half)[123] of funded places.

It is no wonder that olympiads for schoolchildren have also become a hotbed of corruption. Such corrupt practices are similar to the ones of the USE: observers covertly "help" protégés or substitute their works, etc. In some cases even officials of the MES can be involved: in 2012 activist scholars discovered several cases where some names of those persons who even didn't participate in all-Russian olympiads appeared in the lists of these olimpiads' prize-winners confirmed by decrees of the MES[124].

The problem of corruption at olympiads has become so extensive that at the end of 2013 the rector of the Higher School of Economics, Iaroslav Kuz'minov (who is considered to be one of the most influential promoters of Russian higher education reforms), stated that many olympiads are corrupted and offered the MES to oblige prize-winners to take the relevant USE exam and to get not less than a 70% score to be admitted to a university. This proposal, however, met with strong opposition from the Union of Russian Rectors, which is the main institutional advocate of keeping olympiads as an al-

---

[122] See, for example: Ivan Medvedev, "Dagestanskiy 'EGE-turizm' – novoe slovo na rynke obrazovatel'nyh uslug," *BFM.ru*, 30 May 2013, http://www.bfm.ru/news/217762 (as of 15 March 2014).

[123] Liubov' Duhanina, "Chestnaia bor'ba ili lazeika dlia korruptsii," *Uchitel'skaya gazeta*, 27 March 2012, http://www.ug.ru/archive/45103 (as of 15 March 2014).

[124] Grigoriy Koliutskii and Leonid Samoilov, "Kak naiti fal'shivyh prizërov olimpiad," *Polit.ru* 21 February 2013, http://polit.ru/article/2013/02/21/quasi/ (as of 15 March 2014).

ternative to the USE[125]. Still, the public reputation of both olympiads and the USE is rather tarnished.

3.3. Cheating

As cheating usually involves some deficit of power compensated for by deception of supervisors, it flourishes mainly at lower levels of a higher education system. The following three forms of cheating—cribbing or resorting to unauthorised hints, plagiarism, and "ghost writing" are the most common.

Given that exams in Russia, in most cases, do not allow the use of reference texts, cribbing or resorting to unauthorised hints typically involves using written cribs, prohibited referring to literature and texts from the Internet, or receiving unauthorised oral hints during exams and interim tests. Until the 1990s, students used handwritten cribs, usually writing them themselves and thus learning and analysing the outlined texts (many students, however, just rewrote cribs composed by someone else). In the 1990s copy machines came into general use and students now had an opportunity to multiply cribs produced by just one person. Besides, some publishing houses, now not being constrained by Soviet censorship and by moral standards, started to publish brochured collections of cribs. Such brochures were available for sale even in some university bookstores.

The widespread use of computers and of the Internet opened a new revolutionary era for cribbing. Now it has become possible to find easily almost any information, copy and paste it, and print it in any format. No reflective reading and analysing of texts used for cribs is now necessary. It opened up a wide range of opportunities even for those students that did not learn at all and knew nothing.

Another kind of opportunity has appeared due to mobile phones: now students can receive unauthorised hints from other people during exams. Mini-headsets made covert communication even easier, especially for stu-

---

125 Aleksandr Chernykh and Elena Lodygina, "Olimpiiskii nezachët," *Kommersant.ru,* 2 December 2013, http://www.kommersant.ru/doc-rm/2357812 (as of 15 March 2014).

dents with long hair who could mask their earpieces more easily. The proliferation of smartphones has also provided new revolutionary opportunities for exam cheating, as now unscrupulous students have got an opportunity both to browse the Internet and to communicate with helpers in writing during exams. Among all, smartphones are actively used this way by unscrupulous school graduates trying to pass the USE tests. As *Rosobrnadzor* did not arrange different tests for examinees in different time zones until 2014, it led to disastrous consequences: those who sat a test first (e.g. school graduates from the Far East) forwarded test questions to those who found correct responses and then, in their turn, placed such responses online for examinees living in the European part of Russia[126].

Expanding access to the Internet made highly important the problem of student plagiarism. More and more students choose to download or copy and paste texts from the Internet instead of writing papers themselves. According to a survey conducted by scholars of the Higher School of Economics, the share of those Russian students who plagiarise in their term and other papers is around 50%[127]. Actually, for a considerable part (if not for a majority[128]) of students the process of studying turns into mechanical copying and pasting texts from the Internet while resorting to cribbing and unauthorized hints during exams. For such students, extensive collections of papers are available on the Internet both for free or a moderate fee. Together with plenty of opportunities for cribbing, this means that unscrupulous students enrolled in many programmes (especially in some social science and humanities programs) are more likely to be able to graduate from their universities without acquiring any significant new knowledge in comparison to that they acquired in a secondary school.

The situation with plagiarism among teaching staff is not much better. Some of them, as already mentioned, deliver to students lectures consisting

---

126 "EGE doviol Medvedeva do chasovyh poiasov," *Rambler.ru*, 27 May 2013, http://new s.rambler.ru/19269037/ (as of 1 April 2014).
127 Irina Ivoilova, "Ukradennye mysli," *Rossiiskaia gazeta*, 20.01.2009, http://www.rg.ru/2 009/01/20/referaty.html/ (as of 1 April 2014).
128 In late 2008 I checked for plagiarism in essays by more than 100 students of the "Area Studies" and "International Relations" majors, studying in one of the universities in the city of Volgograd. Plagiarism was found in more than two third of all cases.

of text portions (including even portions of texts from student papers available online) borrowed from the Internet. Plagiarism in academic works is also widespread; ironically, in September 2012, while examining 22 articles on corruption in the Russian higher education system (uploaded from the largest Russian articles database elibrary.ru) I managed to find plagiarism in four of these papers without making any special searching efforts.

Though formally plagiarism is a serious offence punishable by the Russian Criminal Code, it is difficult to punish unscrupulous academics or students, as punishment is provided only in cases when "this act has caused heavy damage to the author or another possessor of right."[129] If the damage was not heavy or if it was not an author or another possessor of the rights but some third party (e.g. a university) that was damaged, a person who borrowed a text illegitimately will likely not be punished (that includes nearly all typical cases when a text is plagiarised for somebody's thesis by voluntary consent of this text's true author). Moreover, juridically plagiarism refers to just literal textual borrowings, not to rewritten text even if it is very close to the original in its meaning.[130] Meanwhile, the use of the term "plagiarism" for accusing somebody can be seriously punished as a false accusation of a crime, if a court does not find such an accusation formally correct.

The prevalence of plagiarism is supported by the availability of firms working quite legally and offering their "ghost writing" services (that are also done by independent individuals). Usually former graduates write interim, term, and graduation papers for students, while qualified scholars write C.Sc. and D.Sc. theses, research articles, and monographs for those who would like to obtain C.Sc. or D.Sc. degrees. While for a small fee such firms are ready to produce a paper based on a text plagiarised from the Internet and library books, some "ghost writers" can provide a client with original research, carried out by highly-qualified professionals for a larger fee.

The problem is that the "ghost writing" market is highly competitive and thus prices are rather low: in Moscow a term paper can cost around 40 Euros, a graduate paper—around 200 Euros, C.Sc. thesis—around 1500 Euros,

---

129 *The Criminal Code of the Russian Federation*, Article 146, http://www.russian-criminal-code.com/PartII/SectionVII/Chapter19.html (as of 3 May 2014).
130 Kotliarov and Brumshtein, "Studencheskii plagiat," 31.

D.Sc. thesis—around 5000 Euros. In addition, an "all-in-one" service (including not only writing a thesis itself but also writing and publishing the necessary number of articles; bribing reviewers, some dissertation council members, and experts of VAK) is offered, but its price its significantly higher, e.g. a D.Sc. thesis can cost 10000 Euros or more. In the majority of provincial cities prices can be much cheaper. For a "ghost writer" working in a firm (who does not get all the fee) it is not big money, especially if she or he concentrates on the job completely (sustaining oneself by the money paid for this job) and doing the work slowly, trying to be scrupulous towards the customer. Thus, those "ghost writers" who charge an average market price for their work have a very serious impetus to be unscrupulous towards their clients and to plagiarise, at best just slightly modifying the text (to make plagiarism non-detectable for anti-plagiarism software and search engines) or borrowing texts from monographs or old theses that cannot be found online. At the same time, those who get sufficient money to concentrate on thesis writing during a long time and those who hope to get some intangible benefits from high-standing customers (e.g. subordinates who hope for promotion or researchers who hope for some benefits for their institutions) may do their job quite "scrupulously."

The prevalence and legal character of "ghost writing" services, together with corruption in universities and in the VAK, make it easier for influential officials and business people to obtain a second higher education or a doctoral degree by fraudulent means. It is fashionable for influential people to have several higher education diplomas or a doctoral degree (sometimes both at once)[131] that can be explained by prestigious consumption considerations (that means an official's desire to look more respectable in her/his own eyes

---

131 Many officials obtain them in a random order: many prefer first to defend a thesis and afterwards to obtain a second or third higher education degree. Some achievements of such officials look especially impressive: for example, one senate parliamentary graduated from two universities and received two doctoral degrees between 2003 and 2006. See: Serghei Golunov, "V promezhutkakh mezhdu rabotoy i snom: o geroicheskoi nauchnoi kariere vysokopostavlennykh deputatov," *Troitskii variant* 111 (2012), http://trv-science.ru/2012/08/28/v-promezhutkakh-mezhdu-rabotojj-i-snom-o-geroicheskojj-nauchnojj-karere-vysokopostavlennykh-dissertantov/ (as of 31 March 2014).

and in the eyes of colleagues) and in some cases also by bonuses that are payable by many pubic institutions for having an additional graduate degree or for having a doctoral degree.

As has been revealed thanks to academic activism (to be discussed in the next part of this work) during the last few years, the scope of plagiarism in doctoral theses is so disastrous that the very value of the Russian academic degrees awarding system can be put into serious question. Indeed, the number who have been reasonably accused of dissertation fraud is high not only among officials but also among scholars, including top university managers and heads of departments. The situation looks particularly disastrous regarding some social sciences and humanities (especially economics, law, and political sciences and to a somewhat lesser extent pegagogics and history), as the corresponding degrees are the most popular among unscrupulous officials and business people. This is not to say that the problem is unknown for "non-humanitarian" sciences: as a matter of fact, it also greatly affects the situation with theses in engineering, agricultural, medicine[132], and biology[133]. At the same time, the situation with theses in some other fields, such as philology, mathematics, and physics, is much better as it is very difficult to defend a thesis in such fields for any person who is not very familiar with the text presented for a defence.

It may be argued that many Russian top officials and politicians obtained their doctoral degrees under suspicious circumstances, since the majority of such people supposedly wrote their theses while working simultaneously in positions not related to their research and requiring a full-time presence at a workplace. For example, the head of one of the most powerful Russian corporations, while working at this position, defended his C.Sc. thesis in

---

132 Similar to the salaries of teachers, the salaries of Russian doctors are also very low. As obtaining an academic degree is one of the possible ways to get a salary increase, some doctors try to do this by fraudulent means.

133 In 2013 academic activists accused one university of turning a blind eye to several theses about ground beetles, allegedly based on overwhelmingly the same texts and observation data while just changing regions (e.g. Moldova to Dagestan) where these ground beetles lived. See: Mikhail Gel'fand and Andrei Rostovtsev, "Uchënye zhuzhelitsy Dagestana," *Chastnyi korrespondent,* 14 May 2013, http://www.chaskor.ru/article/uchenye_zhuzhelitsy_dagestana_31972 (as of 31 March 2014).

the MSU in 2005 and his D.Sc. thesis in the same university in 2007[134]. Similarly, a governor of a province, while working in this capacity, defended his C.Sc. thesis in 1997 and D.Sc. thesis in 1999; notably, both dissertations were defended in a university situated in the capital of the province, which was governed by the very same person[135]. In the second case, such a strange academic biography was not an obstacle for members of the RAS to elect this person as a corresponding member first and a full member several years after. Last but not least, in 2006 Russian President Vladimir Putin himself was accused by U.S. researchers of plagiarising in his thesis defended in 1997[136]; it is worth noting that he worked at full-time official positions during and long before this.

To estimate the share of suspicious degrees obtained by Russian top officials, I analysed in 2012 biographies of all the Federal Assembly (Russian bicameral parliament) and Security Council members, ministers, and heads of regions at that time. Degrees obtained by such officials were qualified as dubious if at least two of the three following characteristics were present: 1) evident inconsistency between a dissertation's research domain and a defender's major; 2) during several years immediately prior to her or his defence an official held a labour-intensive position requiring a full-time presence at a workplace; and 3) absence of an official's publications (not counting the thesis itself and publications likely written to qualify for defending the thesis) in the databases of the Russian State Library (www.rsl.ru) and the Scientific Electronic Library (www.elibrary.ru)[137]. The author's task was not so much in obtaining precise figures, but rather in providing a minimal realistic estimate of the prevalence of the considered practice. That is why the wording "at least" is stressed in some cases.

The analysis revealed that 51% of considered top officials and politicians had doctoral degrees. Degrees in economics were the most popular:

---

134 See: *Russian State Library*, http://goo.gl/tFyLrp (as of 31 March 2013).
135 See: *Russian State Library*, http://goo.gl/91ajEl (as of 31 March 2013).
136 "Researchers Peg Putin as a Plagiarist over Thesis," *Washington Post,* 24 March 2006, http://www.washingtontimes.com/news/2006/mar/24/20060324-104106-9971r/ (as of 5 May 2014).
137 The figures on dubious dissertations given are published in: Golunov, "V promezhutkakh."

43% of high-ranking degree holders had them, while only about 15% had the second most popular degree that was one in law, 9% had degrees in engineering and 6% had degrees in political sciences. At least 47% of all theses were obtained under dubious circumstances according to at least two criteria presented above; additionally, some 13% of the other degrees raise "moderate" suspicion according to one of the three criteria[138]. By discipline, the share of suspicious theses is nominally the greatest in the field of psychology (71%) but the overall share of degree holders in this field (1.7%, or in absolute figures seven degree holders) was very small. Among the holders of doctoral degrees in the most popular field of economics the share of suspicious cases was estimated to be the second largest (63%). Among theses in political sciences 58% can be considered dubious, in sociology 56%, in law 45%, in history 44%, and in philosophy and technical sciences[139] 25% in the each case.

Though informally academics do not believe the authenticity of the majority of such officials' academic degrees, it does not have a serious impact on these officials' reputations. Moreover, higher education institutions or academic associations often seek their friendship hoping to obtain funding and protection. That is why officials having dubious academic degrees are gladly invited to make reports at plenary sessions of academic events (in such cases there is usually no possibility to ask questions) or to take up senior positions in academic associations. Prominent officials, including those who have suspicious academic backgrounds, are gladly accepted to teaching or even mid-level administrative positions (heads of departments or deans) by many Russian universities, including the leading ones.

Not only officials but also many of those who occupy senior positions in the higher education system defended their dissertations under dubious circumstances. In 2013 I made an evaluation of the circumstances under which 694 current university rectors[140] defended their theses, using the same crite-

---

138 The dissertations, which arouse just "mild" suspicion, will not be taken into account in the further calculations concerning suspicious theses.
139 These results probably can be explained by a director of a factory or an agricultural firm potentially having a wide range of possibilities to expropriate the inventions of her or his subordinates.
140 Actually I analysed the biographies of 1060 rectors but in only 694 cases was I able to find the relevant information about their academic careers.

ria that I used for evaluation of top officials' dissertations. According to my estimation based on biographical analysis, at least about 10 percent of these rectors (including those of some federal universities and of other universities having special status) obtained their academic degrees under such suspicious circumstances (especially while holding labour intensive full-time official positions). As mentioned in the previous chapter, the practice of appointing prominent retired officials as rectors by the MES or other ministries in some cases is similar to the infeudation practices of the Middle Ages, in which the university plays the role of feud that has been granted to such an official for her or his previous service.

Recent revelations by academic activists put into serious doubt the original character of dissertations written by the heads of some prestigious universities, including federal universities[141], other state universities[142], and of an institute that is a branch of the MSU[143], etc. In November 2013 academic activists accused some high-standing officers from the MES of using large chunks of illicitly borrowed texts from previous works in their theses[144].

---

141 See for example: Viktoria Gabysheva, "Teoria I praktika plagiata," *Vesti Iakutii,* 14 June 2013, http://www.vesti14.ru/articles/523/849/?sphrase_id=750 (as of 31 March 2014); Viktoria Gabysheva, "Teoria I praktika plagiata - 5, ili ptichka na vetke – ne burunduk," *Vesti Iakutii,* 12 July 2013, http://www.vesti14.ru/articles/523/845/?sphrase_id=750 (as of 31 March 2014).

142 See for example: "Astapov Mikhail Borisovich," *Dissernet.org,* http://www.dissernet.org/expertise/astapov.htm (as of 31 March 2013); Dissernet.org, "Fediakina Lidia Vasilievna," http://www.dissernet.org/expertise/fedyakinalv2009.htm (as of 31 March 2014); "Pupkov Sergei Viktorovich," *Dissernet.org,* http://www.dissernet.org/expertise/pupkovsv2010.htm (as of 31 March 2014); "Shvetsov Mikhail Nikolaievich," *Dissernet.org,* http://www.dissernet.org/expertise/schvetsovmn2009.htm (as of 31 March 2014).

143 "Abylgaziev Igor' Ishenalievich," *Dissernet.org,* http://www.dissernet.org/expertise/abylgazievii2005.htm (as of 31 March 2014). It is worth noting that, being quite aware of these accusations, the Academic Council of this institute found it possible to elect this person a director even though the accusations were not refuted convincingly. See: Askol'd Ivanchik, "Vostokovedy MGU vybrali sebe direktora: im stal polkovnik v otstavke i 'klient' 'Disserneta'," *Ekho Moskvy,* 13 January 2014, http://www.echo.msk.ru/blog/a_ivanchik/1237112-echo/ (as of 31 March 2014).

144 "'Dissernet' nashiol plagiat v nauchnyh rabotah vysokopostavlennykh chinovnikov Minobrnauki," *Obschaia gazeta,* 14 November 2013, http://www.og.ru/news/2013/11/14/71490.shtml (as of 31 March 2014).

Among those rectors who were accused by academic activists of improper borrowing from other authors' earlier texts, was the person that succeeded to the rector's post in the National University of Science and Technology "MISIS"[145] from the current minister of Education and Science Dmitrii Livanov, who positions himself as a reformer and a fighter against corruption and fraud. As a former rector of this university who became the minister immediately after holding this post, Dmitrii Livanov probably had a very strong influence over choosing his successor with a rather non-typical academic background for being qualified for this position: this person had just a C.Sc. degree in economics, and the topic of her thesis was not related with steel and alloys, in which this university specialises.

In addition to this, in 2012-2014 there was a series of high-profile scandals involving the dissertation councils of some leading Russian universities, individual scholars working as members of such councils, and in some cases experts of the VAK: these councils and individuals were accused either of deliberate sheltering dissertation fraud or of professional impropriety.

The first of these scandals involved the dissertation council for History of the Moscow State Pedagogical University: after revelations by academic activists an expert commission of the MES in 2012 found that authors of 24 theses defended at this council referred to non-existent publications in the lists of their research works and that authors of some of these theses had plagiarised. As a result of this investigation, the degrees of 11 persons defended in this council were cancelled by the VAK, the council itself was dissolved, and the chairman of the council and later the rector of the university were fired. While justifying these harsh measures the Minister of Education and Science Dmitrii Livanov called the dissertation council for history of the MSPU "a factory producing false theses."[146]

---

145 "Chernikova Alevtina Anatolievna," *Dissernet.org,* http://www.dissernet.org/expertise /chernikovaaa2008.htm (as of 31 March 2014).
146 "Komissia Minobrnauki nashla 'massovye falsifikatsii' s dissertatsiiami, v tom chisle plagiat u glavy SUNTs MGU," *Gazeta.ru,* (31 January 2013), http://www.gazeta.ru/ science/news/2013/01/31/n_2732537.shtml (as of 31 March 2014); "MGPU ob"avil ob uvol'nenii predsedatelia dissertatsionnogo soveta," *Lenta.ru,* 2 February 2013, http://lenta.ru/news/2013/02/02/danilov/ (as of 31 March 2014).

Academic activists using software specially invented for systematic plagiarism checks by Andrei Rostovtsev, have launched, since 2013, a systematic audit of theses defended in Russia during the last decade[147], and they found some other academic centres distinguished by especially high numbers of suspicious theses defended in their dissertation councils. According to the interim results, calculated by Rostovtsev in January 2014, such well-known and respectable academic centres as RANEPA (former Russian Academy of State Service), MSPU, Russian State Humanitarian University, Saint Petersburg State University of Engineering and Economics[148], and MSU were in the "top five" of this "rating" of dubious achievements[149]. Such data does not mean that these universities as a whole were suspected of assisting dissertation fraud, in all cases there were one or several specific dissertation councils that made crucial contributions to their universities' positions in this infamous rating.

Systematic anti-plagiarism checks for "dissertation factories" targeted not only universities and their dissertation councils but also expert councils of the VAK, consisting of experts in various disciplines and responsible for approving results of theses defences in universities. Despite the VAK essentially renewing its expert councils in 2013, allegedly so they only consisted of experts with untarnished reputations, in 2014 activists determined that many of them were research advisors of between one to six highly suspicious theses[150]. After a scandal broke out, the head of the VAK, Vladimir Filippov, had to promise that recently appointed members of expert councils would be re-

---

147 The electronic library of theses of the Russian State Library contains predominantly only those theses that were defended since 2002. It narrows the scope of those theses that could be checked automatically.
148 In 2012 it merged with another university and became Saint Petersburg State University of Engineering and Economics.
149 Andrei Rostovtsev, "Stanesh' doktorom nauk, ne slezaia s svoi verbliud," *LiveJournal* (11 January 2014), http://afrikanbo.livejournal.com/349002.html (as of 1 April 2014).
150 Aleksei Khokhlov, "Iz ekspertnykh sovetov VAK predlozhili iskliuchit' figurantov rassledovanii 'Disserneta'," *Lenta.ru*, 12 February 2014, http://lenta.ru/news/2014/02/12/sovet/ (as of 1 April 2014); Sergei Parkhomenko, "Ministr Livanov nikak ne otnositsia," *Colta.ru*, 11 February 2014, http://www.colta.ru/articles/specials/2006 (as of 1 April 2014).

placed if the suspicions were proven[151]. However, no clear mechanism that will allow the avoidance of those experts, who previously contributed systematically to successful defences of plagiarised theses, has been offered yet.

3.4. Consequences

The pervasiveness of malpractice has a wide range of consequences, and probably not all of these consequences are entirely negative. For instance, it can be argued that in the 2000s corruption has become a powerful incentive for infrastructure modernisation in universities, since after the introduction of the USE (which sharply diminished the importance of shadow incomes from enrolees for university top managers) kickbacks from construction and repair works and equipment procurement became especially important sources of shadow income for corrupted university managers. While it would be a mistake to use corruption to exclusively explain the boom in construction and renovation works and purchases of equipment experienced by many universities in the 2000s in contrast to the "poor 1990s," this factor should be taken into account very seriously.

Yet, the negative impact of malpractice clearly outweighs such positive effects. The main problem is that malpractice leads to the devaluation of Russian higher education, since there is no guarantee that a diploma or a degree was not obtained due to the systematic use of various malpractices. Those who try to pass the USE fairly, without receiving unauthorised hints or bribing supervisors, seriously risk of being less competitive in comparison to those who cheat. Numerous students who get positive marks due to the systematic use of plagiarism, unauthorised hints, cribbing, bribing, or connections, have a good chance to graduate university with virtually the same level of knowledge that they had before enrolling at university. Taking also into account that in many universities half or even more of the students plagiarise systematically, one can speculate that the extent to which devaluation of di-

---

151 "Glava VAK poobeshchal zamenit' ekspertov komissii, esli budut somnenia v ih reputatsii," *Newsru.com*, 13 February 2014, http://www.newsru.com/russia/13feb2014/vak.html (as of 1 April 2014).

plomas occurs is probably close to catastrophic. As a result, the mechanisms of selecting future elites according to the criteria of skills and competence are degraded. All of this also even concerns such vitally important spheres as medicine, engineering, and computer technology, where incompetence can lead to especially grave consequences.

In a similar way, devaluation concerns Russian doctoral degrees: many of which were obtained by those who resorted to plagiarising and hiring "ghost writers." Those who got doctoral degrees by fraudulent means occupy important positions at all levels of the Russian higher education system itself. There are alarming trends of appointing influential retired officials (many of whom probably did not write their theses themselves) to high-paid top managerial positions in prestigious universities or of electing high-standing acting officials of this kind to be heads of academic professional associations. After achieving such positions, those officials who obtained their degrees by fraudulent means are able not only extract income by fraudulent means when possible, but also dictate academic communities to use their rules of the game, neglecting principles of academic integrity.

The pervasiveness of malpractice in universities normalise corruption and cheating in the eyes of students, teaching them "that cheating and bribing is an acceptable way to advance their careers; that personal effort and merit do not count; and that success comes rather from favouritism, manipulation and bribery."[152] While since the 2000s bureaucrats and politicians have being trying to make students "more moral" by requiring higher education institutions to "strengthen upbringing work" (primarily patriotic upbringing), the pervasiveness of malpractices mean these efforts are in vain, as this pervasiveness corrupts the younger generation and contributes to the acceptance and adoption of patterns of unscrupulous behaviour by youngsters. According to some research, Russian students are even more tolerant to corruption than young people who do not study at universities[153]. There is a real threat that such students could become a "lost generation" that can hardly be relied on in

---

[152] Hallak and Poisson, *Corrupt Schools*, 56.
[153] Rimskii, "Sposobstvuet li"; Kirill Titayev, "Pochëm ekzamen dlia naroda? Etiud o korruptsii v vysshem obrazovanii," *Ekonomicheskaya sotsiologiya* 6:2 (2005): 80.

the course of modernisation and anti-corruption reforms that Russia needs badly.

Widespread corruption also means a waste of resources allocated to higher education[154]. Funding the education of those students who do not really study or of those candidates for doctoral degrees who plagiarise or resort to the help of "ghost writers" looks to be meaningless. Large-scale embezzlement in the higher education system, among all, deprives the system of the money that could be used for paying decent salaries to Russian university teachers. As a result of collusion between university managers and suppliers, universities receive less goods and services, or goods and services of a lower quality[155].

3.5. Conclusion

Malpractice in the sphere of Russian higher education is generally not something peculiar or untypical: the overwhelming majority of such malpractice is well-known worldwide. What is less typical is the deep rootedness of the malpractice at all levels of the system to such an extent that some malpractices (e.g. cribbing, plagiarism, and clientelism) seriously threaten to make the educational process meaningless and to devaluate diplomas that certify the validity of qualifications obtained by graduates or by those who defend their doctoral theses.

Such pervasiveness of the above-mentioned corruption and cheating practices can be explained by the cumulative effect of trends and factors considered in the previous chapter. For instance, the general inefficiency of efforts to stop plagiarism and cribbing can be attributed to massivisation (that makes it more difficult to control students), to marginalisation of a teacher's status (that deprives the teacher of motivation to control students efficiently), to bureaucratisation (that both emphasises the importance of good indices and distracts university managers from solving problems considered "sec-

---

154 Hallak and Poisson, *Corrupt Schools*, 55-56.
155 Ibid., 56.

ondary" from a bureaucratic point of view), and to growing authoritarianism suppressing undesirable grassroots initiatives and bringing too principled teachers down a peg. Challenges posed by factors external to the higher education system, such as the ubiquity of the Internet and of cell phones, are also of crucial importance.

All of this does not mean that all Russian universities are hopelessly corrupted and especially that all university teachers resort to malpractice. As a matter of fact, the prevalence of malpractice may vary significantly depending on the specific university or on its specific unit. It is also important that some measures targeting malpractice are taken periodically at various levels of the Russian higher education system. These measures and their outcomes will be examined in the next chapter.

4 COUNTERACTION EFFORTS

While Russian malpractice in the sphere of higher education has no significant national specificity, the efforts undertaken by various governmental and non-governmental actors to combat corruption and cheating, as well as the results obtained due to these efforts, are much more specific. Though such measures often lack consistency and vigour, it would not be just to argue that no significant efforts to combat corruption in the Russian higher education have been made. Actually, the MES once and again tries to tighten its control over those institutions and relations that are especially vulnerable to malpractice, while online academic activism makes a more and more important contribution to exposing cases of corruption and cheating in the 2010s.

I will start this part by considering typical best practices that are employed to combat corruption and cheating in higher education worldwide. After this I will focus on the efforts undertaking by Russian official institutions, primarily by governmental agencies and universities. Then the next section is devoted to the rapidly developing phenomenon of online activism that over recent years has taken on particularly great importance in terms of combatting dissertation fraud. Finally, I will try to estimate the extent to which foreign and international institutions could contribute to reducing the scope of corruption and cheating in the Russian higher education system.

4.1. Strategies and best practices

The key common aspect in policy-oriented works that are devoted to the struggle with malpractice in education is that there are no isolated measures that can improve the situation cardinally and that an integrated approach is needed. Moreover, educational anti-corruption reforms may be inefficient if they target only the educational sector without being supported by reforming anti-corruption legislation, management of the civil service, rules of procurement, regulations of disbursement, transfer, and use of public funds, etc.[156]

Taking this reservation into account, I will try to categorise those practices that are employed for combatting corruption and cheating in the sphere of higher education worldwide. No claims are made for the highly original character of this section, and I will try mostly to summarise the relevant results of the project "Ethics and Corruption in Education" conducted in the 2000s and largely represented in Hallak and Poisson's book[157]. To conceptualise in brief the best practices considered in this book and in other works I will merge them into the four following groups of approaches: 1) repression and prohibition; 2) improving norms and management; 3) stimulating public control; and 4) training and motivating those who are struggling with malpractice. Some of the relevant measures could be attributed to two or more of these approaches at once.

Repressions and prohibitions aim at punishing or deterring violators, prohibiting practices that create fertile ground for corruption (e.g. practices that lead to conflicts of interest), and strengthening law enforcement control over vulnerabilities (such as procedures of examination or budgetary spending). For instance, some countries take demonstratively tough measures against fraud at entrance examinations: e.g. in some countries special services or the army are used to maintain order and ensure strict control[158]. Various sanctions and forms of punishment, based not only on national legislation but also on universities' internal norms (e.g. on norms of ethic codes) are used. Some offences (such as forging diplomas, bribe-taking or bribe-giving, or embezzlement) can be punished by imprisonment, expulsion from a university, imposing a fine, and cancelling results of exams or tests. It is important, on the one hand, that punishments are not excessively harsh and pitiless if some significant mitigating circumstances are found while, on the other hand, the proclaimed penalties can be really implemented and they do not just remain on paper.

---

156 See for example: Hallak and Poisson, *Corrupt schools*, 24.
157 Hallak and Poisson, *Corrupt schools*.
158 Eckstein, *Combating academic fraud*, 58.

Improving norms and management prioritises institutional reforms, intended primarily to reduce opportunities for malpractice. Such reforms could be aimed at introducing efficient and simple norms and procedures (e.g. rules of budgetary and procurement control, ethical codes, and anti-plagiarism policy), clear delineation of responsibilities between supervisory bodies, establishing clear criteria of competitive selection (e.g. for staff and suppliers), exclusion of actors that have bad reputations (such as unscrupulous suppliers or applicants for positions), making it useless to plagiarise or receiving unauthorised hints (e.g. by using creative assignments for exams), automating reporting procedures, and encouraging feedback from staff and students.

It is important that norms and best practices should not only be introduced but also enforced and that reforms should take into account the reactions of perpetrators of malpractices, who often manage to adjust to changing circumstances quickly. Thus, large-scale sectorial reforms should be supported by periodical evaluation of intermediate results, e.g. by performing risk analysis or SWOT analysis, or conducting sociological surveys[159]. At the university level, the problem of enforcement especially concerns ethical codes, which in theory should be a crucially important tool for maintaining academic integrity and for preventing and punishing academic misconduct, but actually often remain largely just on paper for various reasons: complexity, poor awareness by staff of their contents, and lack of mechanisms allowing decision-making on their basis[160]. There is also a danger that ethical codes (especially under the conditions of non-democratic university governance) can be used selectively for score-settling and for repressions rather than for improving the academic environment[161]. To prevent all of this it is recommended

---

159 For greater details concerning the application of such methods for evaluating relevant risks and vulnerabilities see: Hallak and Poisson, *Corrupt Schools*, 72-73, 251.
159 Muriel Poisson, *Corruption and Education*, Education policy booklet series No. 11 (Paris: International Institute for Educational Planning, 2010), 18.
160 Muriel Poisson, *Corruption and Education*, Education policy booklet series No. 11 (Paris: International Institute for Educational Planning, 2010), 18.
161 B.P. Khandelwal, "Teachers' codes of practice in South Asia: comparative analysis of their design, implementation and impact in Bangladesh,India (Uttar Pradesh) and Nepal," in Jacques Hallak and Muriel Poisson, eds, *Governance in education:transparency and accountability* (Paris: International Institute for Educational Planning, 2006), 165.

to make the norms simple and unambiguous, to inform staff and students about these norms properly, to entrust implementation to a body independent from university top managers, and to maintain an open database on cases of punishable misconduct[162].

One of the key directions of debates concerning anti-corruption educational reforms is discussing the centralisation versus decentralisation dilemma. On the one hand, decentralising the system by increasing autonomy and powers of various bodies (e.g. of universities, their departments, bodies controlling financial operations of universities, ethics committees, bodies responsible for controlling entrance examinations, and bodies specially responsible for anti-corruption investigations) could make the system more flexible, transparent, and resistant to corruption pressure from higher authorities within the higher education system. As Hallak and Poisson argue, centralised and over-bureaucratised systems are often slow and heavily dependent on information received from subordinate bodies; as a result, their norms and orders can be easily circumvented by those who would like to exploit such systems' weaknesses. On the other hand, a decentralised system may become less manageable when drastic anti-corruption reforms are needed and more vulnerable to pressure by local influential actors[163]. Thus, some experts argue that decentralisation probably should be considered not as a panacea but rather just an initial step in the right direction that should be combined with reforms increasing the capacity of both central and local bodies[164].

Stimulating public control involves increasing the informational transparency of a higher education system's functioning and encouraging public control (e.g. control by students, parents, and non-commercial organisations) over this system. It is important not only to ensure broad access to budgetary, procurement, and other key information about the work of educational institutions but also to promote public awareness about the right to access such information, to make this information easily understandable, and to provide var-

---

162 Ibidem.
163 Hallak and Poisson, *Corrupt schools*, 165.
164 Ibid., 70.

ious opportunities to give feedback by those activists who detect violations[165]. The experience of some European post-socialist countries, which took serious efforts to combat corruption, demonstrate that anti-corruption student movements (such as the Bosnian "Millenium" [166] or international Anti-Corruption Student Network in South East Europe[167]) can counteract normalisation of corruption and cheating among students and the public in general and encourage governments and NGOs to join such movements' initiatives.

It should be taken into account that even very good norms, mechanisms, and procedures may not work without proper *training and motivating of those who are involved in struggling with malpractice*. Anti-corruption education that promotes academic integrity and activism could target not only managers, teachers, and students, but also activists of non-governmental organisations and the public as a whole[168]. In particular, it is important to teach them the skills of anti-corruption monitoring of budgetary expenditures and of supplier selection procedures.

Again, probably none of the mentioned types of measures alone is sufficient for achieving serious success in combatting educational malpractice: repressive measures without eradicating the roots of the problem would likely just stimulate more sophisticated malpractice, while even very good norms may not work without their proper implementation that should likely be based on autonomy, initiative, competence, and integrity of the participating actors. Finally, it is difficult to implement an integrated approach in a hostile social and political environment that would likely resist reforms making them half-hearted at best.

---

165 Jacques Hallak and Muriel Poisson, "Synthesis and conclusions," in Jacques Hallak and Muriel Poisson, eds, *Governance in education:transparency and accountability* (Paris: International Institute for Educational Planning, 2006), 393.
166 "Bosnia and Herzegovina. A 'Copy-and-Paste' Approach to University Success," in Bettina Meier and Michael Griffin, eds, *Stealing the Future. Corruption in the Classroom. Ten Real World Experiences* (Berlin: Transparency International, 2005), 25-26.
167 See: *Anti-corruption Student Network in South-East Europe*, http://see-corruption.net/
168 Hallak and Poisson, *Corrupt schools*, 283.

4.2. Official efforts

A resolute struggle with corruption and cheating in higher education can hardly be considered a key priority for the Russian government and for the overwhelming majority of universities, which in the 2010s are prioritising the rather formal "criteria of efficiency," such as budgetary income per capita, amount of expenditures per student, number of graduates who found jobs related to their specialities, and number of scientific publications, etc.[169] Nevertheless, it would definitely be not fair to say that nothing is being done to combat malpractices, as actually a lot of measures are being taken. Law enforcement bodies arrest bribe-taking university managers and many bribe-taking university teachers annually. The government strengthens its control over various spheres of university management, makes universities and dissertation councils publish a large amount of information online, and tries to prevent exam and dissertation fraud. Universities try to defend their students from extortion, some struggle vigorously against the giving of unauthorised hints during exams and against plagiarism.

The bureaucratisation of the 2000s-2010s (already considered in the second chapter) has been aimed at, among other things, preventing abuses of power by university managers. As a result, universities' financial and property management activities are under much stricter control by the MES and by law enforcement bodies than in the 1990s (though universities' extra-budgetary expenditures are still monitored less thoroughly than budgetary expenditures), while rectors have become much more dependent on higher authorities and now could be fired under various pretexts.

Since the second half of the 2000s Russia has tried to bring its legislation in line with international anti-corruption norms. Among such norms is the declaring of incomes by officials and their closest relatives (spouses and minor children). Though already in 2009 holders of Russian public posts were obliged to declare their incomes, rectors resisted declaring or at least making

---

169 "Primernyi perechen' kriteriev otsenki effektivnosti deiatel'nosti vysshikh uchebnykh zavedenii," *Samarskiy gosudarstvennyi tekhnicheskiy universitet*, 12 June 2012, http://uup.samgtu.ru/sites/uup.samgtu.ru/files/20120716185408.pdf (as of 5 April 2014).

their declarations public under various pretexts: for instance, in November 2011 the MES responded to activists that rectors of SPSU and MSU are not required to declare their income inasmuch as the universities were founded in the 18th century by the emperor Peter I and the empress Elizabeth I, respectively, and not by the government of the Russian Federation that has issued the decree[170]. In 2013 the overwhelming majority of rectors ignored the order of the Minister of Education and Science Dmitrii Livanov to publish income declarations on respective universities' sites[171]. Finally, this information, demonstrating the huge gap between the salaries of rectors and ordinary university teachers, was published by the MES itself on its site in June 2013[172]. However, only the information about those 300 rectors whose universities were directly subordinated to the MES was made public, while similar information about the incomes of rectors from universities that are subordinated to other agencies is still mostly not known.

As mentioned in the previous chapter, the introduction of the USE in the 2000s was aimed at, among other things, preventing corruption during entrance exams. Despite numerous vulnerabilities that have become evident, the government and the MES resist the demands of numerous critics whom propose the USE should be abolished. Instead the MES tries to improve it, making the USE, among other things, more resistant to corruption and cheating. Numerous helplines for examinees were opened by local branches of the MES and of other official agencies in the 2010s. In February 2014 *Rosobrnadzor* announced that additional security measures will be introduced to ensure fair results: separate versions of tests will be designed for various time zones, tests will be delivered to examination points by governmental couriers, exam papers will be checked outside those regions where they were written, and video surveillance over exams will become mandatory[173].

---

170 See: *Universant.info*, http://universant.info/img/predvibor1.pdf (as of 5 April 2014).
171 "Rektory opublikuiut deklaratsii o dokhodah na saitakh vuzov," *RIA Novosti*, 24 March 2013, http://ria.ru/society/20130324/928743334.html (as of 5 April 2014).
172 "Svedenia o dokhodakh", *The Ministry of Science and Education of the Russian Federation*.
173 Aleksandr Chernykh, "EGE rasfasuiut v pakety," *Kommersant*, 20 February 2014, http://www.kommersant.ru/doc/2412517 (as of 5 April 2014).

Some measures have been taken to combat dissertation fraud. In 2001 the VAK introduced a list of journals in which degree seekers had to publish results of their studies to be qualified to defend their theses. Initially, publishing in such journals was mandatory for applicants for the D.Sc. degree and since 2007 also for the applicants for the C.Sc. degree. The number of articles that applicants had to publish in journals on "the list of the VAK" before defending their theses increased dramatically over time: for the C.Sc. degree from 1 to 3 and for the D.Sc. degree from 3 to 15.

Yet it became clear very quickly that "the list of the VAK" serves as a barrier against conscientious thesis defenders rather than against those unscrupulous degree seekers who did not write their theses themselves. A very large number of weak journals were included on the list due to powerful lobbyists. Many, if not a significant majority, of those journals that were included on the list started to charge rather expensive sums for publications and were ready to publish almost anything for money. Thus, "the list of the VAK" actually turned from a barrier against unscrupulous applicants to a new source of corruption[174].

After a scandal with a "dissertation factory" in MSPU broke out, referred to in the previous part, the MES and the VAK took more resolute steps to combat dissertation fraud. A special commission was created by the MES to investigate the case and 11 degrees (6 D.Sc. degrees and 5 C.Sc. degrees) were cancelled by the VAK following this investigation[175]. Following this incident and other numerous dissertation fraud scandals, in September 2013 the Russian government adopted new rules for the awarding of academic degrees. These rules increased the term of appeal against decisions on awarding C.Sc. and D.Sc. degrees from three to ten years, obliged applicants and dissertation councils to publish full texts of theses on the Internet, clearly mentioned plagiarism and the inclusion by applicants of non-existent publica-

---

174 See for example: Natalia Dëmina, "Spisok VAK kak zerkalo rossiiskoi nauki," *Polit.ru*, 7 September 2007, http://polit.ru/article/2007/09/07/spisokvak/ (as of 5 April 2014).
175 "Ministr Livanov lishil 11 chelovek uchionykh stepenei," *RBK Daily*, 12 February 2013, http://rbcdaily.ru/society/562949985775482 (as of 5 April 2014).

tions as grounds for cancelling a degree, and established a detailed procedure of appeal against decisions on awarding doctoral degrees[176].

Yet the measures against dissertation fraud taken by the MES and the VAK were inadequate, as the power of MES was too weak to punish those high-ranking officials whose interests could be threatened by such a campaign. In May 2013 a Deputy Minister of Education and Science, Igor Fediukin, who was the head of the commission investigating the dissertation scandal with MSPU and who gained an informal (maybe somewhat exaggerated) reputation as the most principled fighter against plagiarism in the MES, retired after a vigorous information campaign and attacks by powerful foes were directed against him[177]. Both before and after this resignation virtually none of the cases when high-ranking officials were reasonably accused of plagiarism by academic activists ended with a proper investigation and well-foundedmodified decision. Similarly, before the end of April 2014 there was not even a single case when a university rector, publicly accused of dissertation fraud, was investigated properly and transparently. Yet, on 28 April the rector of the Russian State Social University (a university notorious for having four close relatives in its rectorate) was fired after the expertise of VAK confirmed illegitimate borrowings in her thesis[178]. However, numerous similar cases have still not been investigated properly.

As will be discussed later, the MES does not demonstrate much interest in supporting public activism that can go "too far" in exposing corruption among high-ranking officials. Yet, the Public Council under the MES, which included not only scholars but also independent journalists and other known public figures, was created in 2007 to discuss and evaluate the educational reforms. In 2012 a couple of known political opposition activists (scholar Mi-

---

176 "Postanovlenie Pravitel'stva Rossiiskoi Federatsii ot 24 sentiabria 2013 g. no 842, Moskva, 'O poriadke prisuzhdeniya uchionykh stepenei'," *Vysshaya attestatsionnaia komissia (VAK)*, http://goo.gl/uYdYmz (as of 5 April 2014).
177 "'Borets s plagiatom' Fediukin ushiol s posta zamministra," *Russkaia sluzhba Bi-Bi-Ci*, 28 May 2013, http://www.bbc.co.uk/russian/russia/2013/05/130528_russia_fedyukin_r esignation.shtml (as of 7 April 2014).
178 Andrei Sidorchik, "Semeinoe delo. Za chto uvolili rektora RGSU Lidiu Fediakinu," *Argumenty i Fakty*, 30 April 2014, http://www.aif.ru/society/law/1160417 (as of 1 Mai 2014).

khail Gel'fand and publicist Dmitrii Bykov) were included on this council and a hotline, through which education workers could give feedback to the Council, was established. Since that time the body has become much more active than before: it played an important role in investigating a dissertation scandal in MPSU and repeatedly discussed the issue of dissertation fraud, USE fraud, and overbureaucratisation of education during its sessions[179]. The Council on Science under the MES, established in 2013 and consisting of 22 prominent scholars, also has taken an active public stance: for instance, in February 2014 it publicly demanded that the VAK replace those members of its expert councils who were research advisors on plagiarised theses[180]. Thus, the Public Council and the Council of Science can both influence decisions of the MES and make their voices heard through mass media, though both have done so only to a very limited extent.

Since the 2000s and especially since 2012, when Dmitrii Livanov became the Minister of Education and Science, reforms conducted by the MES have to a considerable extent been based on analytical recommendations by experts of the HSE (a university considered to be one of the leading liberal think tanks in Russia). Though the struggle with corruption and cheating is not among the main priorities of the university's policy-oriented research in the field of education studies, some relevant issues, such as bribery in universities as well as corruption and fraud at the USE, are examined in the framework of the Monitoring of Education Markets and Organisations and some other HSE's projects[181]. One of the potential problems with the HSE's recommendations is that the implementation of proposed reforms (including their effect on the level of corruption and cheating) is also monitored predominantly by the HSE. This can imply conflicts of interest, as the HSE may be not interested so much in emphasising the side effects of the reforms proposed by it.

Anti-corruption and anti-cheating policies pursued by individual universities greatly vary in their scope, vigorousness, and efficiency. Many universi-

---

179 See: *Obshchestvennyi sovet pri Ministerstve obrazovania i nauki Rossiiskoi Federatsii*, http://sovet-edu.ru/work/10 (as of 7 April 2014).
180 "Sovet po nauke prizval MON i VAK peresmotret' sostavy ekspertnykh sovetov," *Gazeta.ru*, 12 February 2014, http://www.gazeta.ru/science/news/2014/02/12/n_594 2229.shtml (as of 7 April 2014).
181 See: *Monitoring ekonomiki obrazovania*, http://memo.hse.ru/ (as of 7 April 2014).

ties have helplines for students, to which cases of bribery and extortion can be reported. Meanwhile, the vast majority of universities, even those that have a special status, have no strict and explicit policies against student cheating and those students, who plagiarise or receive unauthorised hints during exams, usually do not risk being seriously punished for it. Yet a relatively small number of leading state and private universities, such as the European University in St Petersburg[182], HSE[183], MGIMO[184], MSU[185], SPSU[186], and some other universities do have such clear policies, though there is no confidence that these policies are implemented consistently. Among other things, these and some other universities use the commercial version of the most popular online anti-plagiarism service *Antiplagiat,* which was introduced in 2005[187].

The real implementation of strict repressive measures against cheating students requires strong political will from a university's principals who should be ready to, among others, face collective resistance from other students, their parents, and influential lobbyists. In May 2013, after six students of Pirogov Russian National Research Medical University were expelled for giving or receiving unauthorised hints during exams, the current university's rector Andrei Kamkin was attacked not only by parents of these students but also by their university classmates, many of whom signed a petition requiring the restoration of those who were expelled. The pressure was so persistent that it

---

182 "Kodeks akademicheskoi dobrosovestnosti slushatelia i aspiranta EUSPb," *Evropeiskii universitet v Sankt-Peterburge,* http://www.eu.spb.ru/students/the-code-of-academic-integrity (as of 8 April 2014).
183 "Poriadok primenenia distsiplinarnykh vzyskanii pri narusheniakh akademicheskikh norm v napisanii pis'mennykh uchebnykh rabot v Gosudarstvennom universitete – Vysshei shkole ekonomiki," *Natsional'nyi issledovatel'skii universitet "Vysshaia shkola ekonomiki",* http://www.hse.ru/org/hse/antiplagiat_info/plagiat (as of 8 April 2014).
184 "Informatsia o zasedanii Uchënogo soveta universiteta," *MGIMO,* http://goo.gl/Jc6V bG (as of 7 April 2014).
185 "Polozhenie ob obespechenii samostoiatel'nosti vypolnenia pis'mennykh rabot v MGU imeni M.V. Lomonosova na osnove sistemy 'Antiplagiat'," *Moscow State University,* http://goo.gl/KfTHC2 (as of 7 April 2014).
186 "Bor'ba s plagiatom v MGU I v SPbGU," *Sankt-Peterburgskii gosudarstvennyi universitet,* 5 February 2013, http://guestbook.spbu.ru/ru/prorektory-spbgu/lavrikova-marina-yurevna/3164-borba-s-plagiatom-v-mgu-i-v-spbgu.html (as of 7 April 2014).
187 *Antiplagiat,* http://antiplagiat.ru (as of 11 April 2014).

prompted the rector to respond to the students in a very emotional open letter, in which he condemned the appellants for their demands[188].

Since the second half of the 2000s, many of universities have adopted ethical codes, though in the majority of cases they do not really work against those who resort to corruption and cheating. At the same time, some observers have raised their concerns that recently adopted ethical codes are too repressive and can be used against dissenting teachers or students[189].

Generally, official efforts to combat malpractice in the higher education system can hardly be considered successful. Combatting malpractice is not a top official priority. Instead, the most important priority is making universities efficient according to a large set of formal and measurable criteria. It looks ridiculous, though, that according to such criteria universities can be considered highly efficient while turning a blind eye to corruption and cheating, not actually and systematically punishing plagiarism, not defending their teachers from illicit pressure by those who have more power, paying most of the teachers tiny salaries while maintaining huge academic and bureaucratic workloads, and not encouraging academic mobility. Apart from this, the existing official anti-corruption and anti-cheating policies largely rely on further centralisation and not on maximising information transparency and encouraging university self-governance, feedback, and civic activism.

As a result, official measures for combatting corruption and cheating are often ill-conceived, retarded, frequently implemented by those officers who are themselves corrupt, and they do not target officials who are "too influential."

---

188 "Otkrytoe pis'mo A.G. Kamkina studentam, podpisavshim proshenie o vozvrashchenii v RNIMU im. N.I. Pirogova shesti otchislennykh sokursnikov," *Rossiiskii natsional'nyi issledovatel'skii universitet imeni N.I. Pirogova*, 13 March 2013, http://rsmu.ru/news_rsmu+M5f33f6799fa.html (as of 7 April 2014).
189 Afanasii Krzizanovskii, "Ne pit', ne kurit' I prepodam ne derzit'," *Opengaz.ru*, 12-19 March 2014, http://www.opengaz.ru/issues/09-602/ne-pit-ne-kurit-i-prepodam-ne-der zit.html (as of 7 April 2014); Anna Semenets, "Vuzy poluchat kart-blansh na zachistku?" *Rosbalt*, 26 February 2013, http://www.rosbalt.ru/moscow/2013/02/26/109 9160.html (as of 7 April 2014).

4.3. Academic and student activism

Though Russian activists generally have less power and information than officials, in many cases they prove to be more effective: having information from unique sources and not been reluctant to investigate "senior" officials.

Until the 2010s academic activism in Russia was weak. At the level of individual universities ordinary academics were (and still are) overwhelmingly afraid of conflict with the autocratic university top managers, having no ground to hope for much support from the university trade unions. Even more important, the majority of malpractices are normalised in the eyes of many teachers and students, and the "misprision culture," deeply rooted in Russian society at least since the Soviet time, prevented many teachers from reporting bribery of their colleagues and also prevented the vast majority of students from fighting their fellows' cheating.

Yet in the 2000s there were some activist movements inside individual universities. One of the most well-known movements was the OD Group, which consisted of students from MSU's School of Sociology and actively used not only verbal communication and leaflets but also Internet resources (a site[190] and a LiveJournal blog[191]). The key demand of the OD Group was to reduce prices in a school's café that was allegedly owned by a dean's relative[192]. Other key demands of the group were improving the quality of education and investigating alleged cases of plagiarism by the school's head and some other academics[193]. The group's activity was strongly opposed by the school's leadership who proclaimed dissenting students were paid by some pro-Western forces and extremists who were targeting the existing political order in Russia[194]. The attitudes of the school's other students to the group's

---

190 See the cached version at: See the cached version at: http://web.archive.org/web/20080520053439/http://www.od-group.org/ (as of 9 April 2014).
191 OD Group, http://od-group.livejournal.com/ (as of 9 April 2014).
192 Oleg Kashin, "Shkaf, v kotorom odni skelety," Ekspert Online 14 (2007), http://expert.ru/expert/2007/14/obschestvennoe_dvizhenie/ (as of 9 April 2014).
193 OD Group, "Sostoialas' vstrecha uchastnikov Od-group s rektorom MGU V.A. Sadovnichim," LiveJournal, 3 June 2007, http://od-group.livejournal.com/16716.html (as of 9 April 2014).
194 Kashin, "Shkaf".

activity were diverse: while some supported the group, some supported the school's administration and even proposed expelling the activists for misconduct[195].

In the beginning, the OD Group's activity was rather successful: it managed to obtain support from some academics in the School of Sociology, from other Russian and some foreign academics,[196] and also from some Russian media. Student activists received informal recognition by the MSU's administration: the expensive café was replaced by a much cheaper one and a special university commission for inspecting the quality of education in the School of Sociology was established.

However, in such a large university as the MSU, heads of schools have a very large authoritarian power (in some cases almost comparable to the power of rectors in smaller universities) and that is why even the relatively benevolent attitude to a movement by the university administration[197] could not help the activists to prevail. Ultimately, the OD Group stopped its activities in 2008 after its leaders were expelled from the university for failing to pass exams under controversial circumstances[198] and those who managed to get readmitted by the MSU's administration chose to transfer into another university[199].

Since the end of the 2000s, prerequisites for relatively stable cooperation among adherents of academic integrity from different universities throughout Russia have appeared due to the proliferation of online social networking practices among teachers and students. One such network appeared around the newspaper *"Troitskii variant – nauka,"* which has been published since 2008 both in a printed version and online[200]. The newspaper

---

195 Ibidem.
196 "Pis'ma podderzhki," OD Group, http://web.archive.org/web/20080524081115/http://od-group.org/taxonomy/term/9 (as of 9 April 2014).
197 Sokolov, "Rossiiskii universitet".
198 "Proshla aktsia protesta protiv otchislenia chetyrëkh studentov Sotsfaka MGU," Polit.ru, 27 March 2008, http://www.polit.ru/news/2008/03/27/action/ (as of 9 April 2014).
199 OD Group, "Dvoe iz otchislennykh studentok – aktivistok OD Group vosstanovleny," 5 April 2008, http://web.archive.org/web/20080520053439/http://www.od-group.org/node/677 (as of 9 April 2014).
200 Troitskii variant, http://trv-science.ru/

is funded by the *Dinastia* foundation (headed by a businessman and a scholar Dmitrii Zimin) and the editorial work is done by volunteers. While identifying itself as a newspaper representing the interests of the Russian academic community, "Troitskii variant" encourages the publishing of articles about the acute problems of Russian science and education, including plagiarism and dissertation fraud[201], procurement fraud[202], unfair academic competitions[203], USE fraud[204], overbureaucratisation[205], and autocratic university governance[206] etc. Online versions of the most popular publications are visited thousands of times, and the authors of such publications can be easily reached by like-minded academics from various regions. Apart from this, the newspaper serves as a source of feedback for officers at the MES. The importance of "Troitskii variant" was given de facto recognition by the ministry's leadership: the minister Dmitrii Livanov and his deputy Igor Fediukin attended the newspaper's five year anniversary celebration in April 2013[207].

However, the MES has taken a much less favourable stance towards another academic initiative that focuses on dissertation fraud and exposes many influential figures both in the Russian higher education system and in the Russian political elite. Though individual scandals, involving accusations of high-ranking figures of dissertation fraud, were not something exceptional until the end of 2012[208], revelations have become often and systematic since the very end of that year. Such revelations have become possible largely due to the Russian State Library providing all its customers remote access to its electronic database of theses for a moderate fee starting in 2013.

---

201 See for example: Volkhonskii, "Pokolenie plagiata."; Volikhamov, "MGU i Dissergeit: opasnnye sviazi."
202 See for example: Krushel'nitskii, "Pilite, Shura, pilite."
203 See for example: Onishchenko, "Kormlenie kak sistema."
204 See for example: Ashkinazi, Grishkina, and Ivanova, "Utechka-test."
205 See for example: Ivan Kurilla, "Kriterii otsenki."
206 Vladimir Volkhonskii, "Piatiletka rektora Kropachëva."
207 Natalia Dëmina, "Kak pobedit' fabriki tufty," *Polit.ru,* 6 April 2013, http://www.polit.ru/article/2013/04/06/5years_trv/ (as of 10 April 2014).
208 See for example: "O plagiate v doktorskoi dissertatsii V.R. Medinskogo," *Aktualnaia istoria,* http://actualhistory.ru/medinskyi_plagiat (as of 10 April 2014); "Novosti fonda," *Fond Istoricheskaia pamiat',* 25 May 2011, http://www.historyfoundation.ru/ru/fund_ite m.php?id=148 (as of 10 April 2011).

The first major group targeted by academic activists were members of the Russian parliament belonging to the dominant pro-governmental party United Russia. The most active participants in the campaign, whose revelations are published in their LiveJournal blogs and receive wide publicity[209], were physical scientists Andrei Zaiakin (his LiveJournal nickname was "doct_z") and Andrei Rostovtsev ("afrikanbo") and also journalist Sergei Parkhomenko ("cook"). Apart from them numerous volunteers also took part in checking theses of deputies and other high-ranking officials and politicians.

In January 2013 the initiative took a more organised shape: a voluntary networking community Dissernet was created. Prominent politicians remained its key target, but increasing attention also started to be paid to theses written by scholars working in universities[210] and to revealing the dissertation councils that actually function as "dissertation factories." While activists initially used the online service *Antiplagiat* for detecting plagiarism, later they partially switched to the *"Disserorubka"* ("thesis mincer") software invented by Andrei Rostovtsev, which had important advantages over *Antiplagiat*, as in particular it could check texts (automatically divided into small blocks) via the Yandex search engine[211]. The website of Dissernet, which was opened in September 2013, contained the database of the community's investigations: each suspicious thesis was represented as an interactive clickable table allowing the comparison of text blocks from a suspicious thesis with some earlier identical or very similar texts.

Dissernet relies on various kinds of voluntary assistance: checking theses and other works for plagiarism, surrendering Yandex query quotas[212], and

---

209 See for example: *Doct_z*, "Svoistva i idei, podobnyie blagotvoritel'nym i religioznym abstraktsiyam," *LiveJournal*, 11 January 2013, http://doct-z.livejournal.com/4832.html (as of 10 April 2014); Andrei Rostovtsev, "Iz novostei," *LiveJournal*, 19 February 2013, http://afrikanbo.livejournal.com/296093.html (as of 10 April 2014); Serguei Parkhomenko, "Liudi shokoladnoi lazhi," *LiveJournal*, 7 March 2013, http://cook.livejournal.com/202638.html (as of 10 April 2014).
210 "O soobshchestve," *Dissernet*,http://www.dissernet.org/about/ (as of 11 April 2014).
211 Sergei Parkhomenko, "Veb-mastera i saitovody! Pomogite Dissernetu," *LiveJournal*, 16 September 2013, http://cook.livejournal.com/232078.html (as of 11 April 2014).
212 Sergei Parkhomenko, "Orgomnoe spasibo vam, saitovody i veb-mastera," *LiveJournal*, 17 September 2013, http://cook.livejournal.com/232302.html (as of 11 April 2014).

financial donations, etc. As in the case with "Troitskii variant", Dmitrii Zimin became one of the main sponsors of the community[213].

The activity of Dissernet quickly attracted the attention of the mass media, which willingly reported the cases of high-profile exposures. The community's key figures, such as Andrei Rostovtsev and Sergei Parkhomenko, cooperated with some online media as columnists[214].

At the same time, the activity of Dissernet met with strong resistance from those who were targeted by its exposures. Those who were accused of illegitimate borrowing of some others' texts and their supporters usually chose from the following standard ways of responding: just to keep silent; to call an accusation nonsense and rubbish[215]; to declare an accusation politically motivated[216], non-professional, made by smatterers, and based just on automatic comparison without taking into account various nuances[217] (actually, representatives of Dissernet stressed many times that automatic comparisons are always checked by humans after[218]); to maintain that detected textual concisions are just common phrases used by many authors; or, finally, to declare that only a relevant dissertation council and the VAK have the right to call a

---

213 "O soobshchestve," *Dissernet*, http://www.dissernet.org/about/ (as of 11 April 2014).
214 See for example: "Sergei Parkhomenko," *Echo Moskvy*, http://echo.msk.ru/users/ser guei_parkhomenko/; (as of 30 April 2014); "Andrei Rostovtsev," *Ezhednevnyi zhurnal*, http://www.ej.ru/?a=author&id=433/ (as of 30 April 2014).
215 See for example: "Igor' Lebedev nazval bredom obvinenia v plagiate pri napisanii dissertatsii," *ITAR-TASS*, 18 February 2013, http://itar-tass.com/obschestvo/543082 (as of 11 April 2014); "V press-sluzhbe Astahova otvetili na obvinenia v plagiate," *Vzgliad*, 28 January 2014, http://vz.ru/news/2014/1/28/669960.html (as of 11 April 2014).
216 See for example: "Novyi dissertatsionnyi skandal: u deputata na bukvu 'B' nashli 50% plagiata v nauchnoi rabote," *Newsru.com*, 25 March 2013, http://www.newsru.com/rus sia/25mar2013/batalina.html (as of 11 April 2014).
217 See for example: *Vlast'.zhzh.rf*, "Livanovu ot Levanova," *LiveJournal*, 21 March 2013, http://v1.livejournal.com/95981.html (as of 11 April 2014).
218 Among all, it is explicitly stated in Dissernet's guidance for volunteers. See: *Dissernet*, "Rukovodstvo dlia provedenia samostoiatel'noi ekspertizy po metodike soobshchestva 'Dissernet'," http://www.dissernet.org/instructions/instruction/how-to-do.htm (as of 11 April 2014).

thesis invalid[219]. However, in hardly any cases were clear and concrete responses to the accusations given publicly.

Those who suffered from Dissernet's exposures and their supporters also tried to perform an information counter-attack, unsuccessfully accusing a known academic activist and promoter of Dissernet Mikhail Gel'fand and some officers of the MES of plagiarism or other kinds of academic fraud[220]. They also attacked the *Antiplagiat* online service for its alleged bias towards political opponents[221] and for its monopolistic position in rendering plagiarism-detecting services to universities and other subjects of the Russian higher education system[222].

Although there were virtually no attempts to sue the main public figures of Dissernet, one of the leading Russian newspapers *Novaia Gazeta* and its journalist Nikita Girin were fined approximately 6.6 thousand and 3.3 thousand euros after accusing two judges of the Moscow City Court of plagiarism on the basis of the Dissernet's expertise[223]. The anti-defamation lawsuit, despite the potential conflict of interests, was considered by the very Moscow City Court that refused to order a linguistic comparison of the judges' theses. Neither Andrei Rostovtsev nor Sergei Parkhomenko were put on trial either as witnesses or as co-defendants, despite agreeing to bear responsibility for their accusations[224].

---

219 See for example: *Gazeta.SPb*, "Smol'nyi zaiavil o nekompetentnosti ekspertov po dissertatsii Poltavchenko," (24 May 2013), http://www.gazeta.spb.ru/1210512-0/ (as of 11 April 2014).
220 Anna Popova, "Dissertatsionnye voiny," *Lenta.ru*, 27 April 2013, http://lenta.ru/articles/2013/04/27/empirestrikesback/ (as of 11 April 2014); MG, "Seans s razoblacheniem," *LiveJournal*, 11 February 2013, http://prahvessor.livejournal.com/326776.html (as of 11 April 2014).
221 See for example: *Vlast'.zhzh.rf*, "Livanovu ot Levanova."
222 See for example: *RIA Novosti*, " 'Antiplagiat' ne budet edinstvennym metodom proverki dissertatsii," 22 March 2013, http://ria.ru/science/20130322/928580727.html (as of 11 April 2014).
223 Nikita Girin, "Vash plagiat, Vasha chest'?," *Novaia gazeta*, 11 November 2013, http://www.novayagazeta.ru/politics/60866.html (as of 14 April 2014).
224 "Sud vzyskal s 'Novoi gazety' 410 tysiach rublei za statiu o plagiate," *Newsru.com*, 6 December 2013, http://www.newsru.com/arch/russia/06dec2013/ng.html (as of 14 April 2014).

Some top officers of the MES, rectors of the largest universities, and official figures of the Russian education system also expressed their negative attitudes towards "too radical" anti-plagiarism activism. In April 2013, the Head of the Russian Parliamentary Committee on Education, Viacheslav Nikonov, called for a stop to "these Bacchanalian accusations of anyone of having bogus theses and degrees," as otherwise "we may soon have a situation when all academics will check each other's theses and other works for plagiarism and this may lead even to discretisation of Russian science."[225] Similarly, in June of the same year the rector of MSU, Viktor Sadovnichii, also called for a stop to the "senseless struggle" with dissertation plagiarism that in his opinion was turned into a settling of accounts between adversaries[226].

It is revealing that in February 2014 top officials from the MES made it clear publicly that they need neither cooperation with anti-plagiarism activists nor the results of their expertise. The minister Dmitrii Livanov himself stated that he did not see any value in Dissernet's activity since any conclusion concerning plagiarism "should be made by experts, specialists in corresponding fields of science." Livanov also criticised Dissernet for its allegedly biased approach: he claimed that the community publishes only those results of checks in which plaglarism was found (thus allegedly undermining the reputation of Russian science), that it checks for plagiarism only in theses related to social sciences and humanities, and that it prioritises theses written by politicians and business people, thus politicising the issue[227]. Finally, two weeks later the

---

225 "Viacheslav Nikonov: 'pora zakanchivat' vakkhanaliu s dissertatsiami'," *Radio "Golos Rossii"*, 10 April 2013, http://rus.ruvr.ru/2013_04_10/exvideo-Vjacheslav-Nikonov-Por a-zakanchivat-vakhanaliju-s-dissertacijami/ (as of 12 April 2014).

226 "Sadovnichii: 'bessmyslennaia bor'ba' s fal'shivymi dissertatsiami ne nuzhna," *RIA Novosti*, 20 June 2013, http://ria.ru/society/20130620/944612270.html (as of 12 April 2014).

227 " 'Ia ponimal, chto nado delat' dostatochno serëznye i chasto nepopuliarnye shagi'," *Kommersant*, (10 February 2014), http://www.kommersant.ru/doc/2404422?replyto= 154171036#t154171036 (as of 12 April 2014). All of Livanov's arguments were severely criticised by Andrei Rostovtsev, who particularly stressed that Dissernet does not focus on politicians only and that its activists check theses related to all fields of science. See: Andrei Rostovtsev, "Mifologia Livanova," *Ezhednevnyi zhurnal* (12 February 2014), http://www.ej.ru/?a=note&id=24408 (as of 12 April 2014).

Head of the VAK, Vladimir Filippov, ostentatiously stressed that he never visited the site of the Dissernet as he had no time for this[228].

The results of Dissernet's and other anti-plagiarism activists' revelations seem to be mixed. On the one hand, they definitely managed to attract public attention to the problem and to undermine public respect for those numerous degree holders who defended their theses while occupying high official positions. Moreover, these revelations made evident even for many opponents of the Dissernet that the Russian degree awarding system is rotten and that doctoral degrees have been devalued; that many rectors, deans, heads of departments, and ordinary teachers achieved their current positions due to large-scale academic fraud; and, finally, that urgent reform of the degree awarding system is needed badly. As mentioned in the previous section, on the wave of scandals the government had to make some changes to the procedure of defending doctoral theses, making it, among other things, more transparent for the public. Finally, the struggle with plagiarism greatly contributed to energising academic activism and to attracting new volunteers to it.

On the other hand, in the vast majority of cases, the revelations from Dissernet have not caused academic degrees to be revoked by the VAK or any retirements of high-ranking officials; on the contrary, in virtually no cases has a revelation ruined a career of such an official or became an obstacle for her or his promotion. As discrediting high-ranking officials, politicians, officers of the MES, or rectors could undermine the power of the ruling elite and of key figures in the higher education system, the MES, after a short period of cooperating with activists in the case of the "dissertation factory" in MPSU, started to ignore its revelations, especially when powerful figures were targeted: for instance, in one case when activists of the Dissernet accused a former university rector of copying almost all of his D.Sc. thesis from an a single earlier work, the VAK declined the appeal, issuing a very short formal letter not explaining the reasons for this decision at all[229].

---

228 "Glava VAK priznalsia, chto nikogda ne zakhodil na sait 'Dissernet'," *RIA Novosti*, 27 February 2014, http://ria.ru/science/20140227/997355117.html (as of 12 April 2014).

229 Andrei Rostovtsev, "O vstreche v VshE i ne tol'ko," *LiveJournal*, 8 November 2013, http://afrikanbo.livejournal.com/340768.html (as of 12 April 2014).

It should be also noted that some trends and results of the anti-plagiarism campaign look controversial. First, some accusations of plagiarism look disputable, specifically when it comes to standard phrases from dissertation abstracts used for describing technical tasks or to phrases from jurisprudential thesis based on almost literal paraphrasing of legal provisions: such phrases can be considered a commonplace. Second, activists often used to proclaim that the research supervisors of theses containing plagiarism as accomplices of fraud, which is not necessarily always true: in some cases it would be very difficult for supervisors to detect plagiarism and in some other cases they could just perform their duties negligently, not deliberately contributing to fraud.

Last but not least, the community consists mainly of activists opposed to the ruling regime and to the policy of MES. In many cases revelations predominantly targeted pro-governmental figures or those officials or politicians, who shortly before this did something seriously wrong from the viewpoint of liberal oppositionists. There was also an opposing case when one of the founders of Dissernet defended very aggressively the governor Nikita Belykh (known for his liberal views) from accusations of plagiarism made by researchers holding conservative views[230]; yet, finally Dissernet recognised illegitimate textual borrowings in this governor's thesis[231]. All of this gives reasons not only for Dissernet's opponents but also for some academics (to which the author informally discussed the matter in social networks) to consider the community's activity politically biased. It should be taken into account though that Dissernet is not a centralised community and thus its revelations are not closely coordinated, and also (as stated by one of Dissernet's founders who wrote to the author in the course of an informal discussion) that revelations confined to high profile political events have more chance to have

---

230 Serguei Parkhomenko, "Sluchai Nikity Belykh. Delo zakryto, poiski prodolzhaiutsia," *LiveJournal*, 12 June 2013, http://cook.livejournal.com/218748.html (as of 12 April 2014); Serguei Parkhomenko "Eshchë raz pro Belykh ili 'Obratno pokoinika nesut'...," *LiveJournal,* 26 October 2013, http://cook.livejournal.com/240130.html (as of 12 April 2014).

231 "Belykh Nikita Iur'evich," *Dissernet*, 5 August 2013, http://www.dissernet.org/expertise/belykh.htm (as of 12 April 2014).

wide public resonance. Ultimately, even if selection of "targets" is biased, it does not make reasoned accusations invalid by default.

Some other academic and student organisations have sporadically addressed the problems of corruption and cheating. The *Obshchestvo nauchnykh rabotnikov* (Society of Scientific Workers), founded in 2012 as a grassroots response to unprecedented "alienation of authorities from scientists,"[232] supported anti-plagiarism activists in some of its statements[233] as the struggle with violations of academic integrity is among the Society's key priorities[234]. The Interregional Trade Union of University Workers "*Solidarnost*" ("Solidarity"), founded in 2013 as a really independent alternative to pocket university trade unions, focused on improving some conditions that create favourable grounds for corruption and cheating: protecting the rights of university teachers, raising their salaries, reducing academic workload and student to teacher ratios, promoting university self-governance, and increasing public control over university top management, etc.[235] Yet, Dissernet still remains probably the only Russian public activism initiative that explicitly specialises in combatting some forms of academic corruption or fraud.

4.4. International impact

Corruption and cheating in Russian higher education affects or can affect potentially the interaction of Russian universities and individual researchers with their foreign partners in a number of ways: to undermine mutual trust, to reduce the efficiency of joint projects, and to devalue joint initiatives, etc. For instance, as Heyneman, Anderson, and Nuralieva noticed, recognition of

---

232 "Deklaratsia," *Obshchestvo nauchnykh rabotnikov*, 6 April 2012, http://onr-russia.ru/node/3 (as of 14 April 2014).
233 See for example: "Zaiavlenie Soveta ONR po novomu sostavu ekspertnykh sovetov VAK," *Obshchestvo nauchnykh rabotnikov*, 16 February 2014, http://onr-russia.ru/tags/%D0%BF%D0%BB%D0%B0%D0%B3%D0%B8%D0%B0%D1%82 (as of 14 April 2014).
234 *Obshchestvo nauchnykh rabotnikov*, "Deklaratsia."
235 "Deklaratsia mezhregional'nogo professional'nogo soiuza rabotnikov vysshei shkoly 'Universitetskaia solidarnost' i dva eë proekta," *Universitetskaia solidarnost'*, 25 January 2013, http://unisolidarity.ru/?p=471 (as of 14 April 2014).

equivalence between diplomas, obtained in corrupted universities by dishonest means on the one hand and diplomas of highly-reputable universities on the other hand "would constitute the educational equivalent in the European Union of unilateral disarmament."[236] The range of typical malpractices related to international academic cooperation includes the use of credentials obtained by improper ways in Russia or in other countries[237], "academic tourism," and appropriation and embezzlement of grant funds, etc.[238]

Unfortunately, the capabilities of international and foreign actors to promote academic integrity in the Russian higher education system are very limited. As worldwide experience shows, while the importance of grants and projects of such organisations as UNESCO, the World Bank, and Transparency International is acknowledged, some researchers argue that in many cases international organisations and programs are inclined to turn a blind eye to corruption or feel satisfied with cosmetic measures against corruption so as not to be at loggerheads with recipient countries' governments and not to provoke governmental disappointment towards such institutions' activities[239].

Though the Bologna Process, in which Russia participates, employs external evaluation of participating universities' performance[240] and has quality

---

236 Heyneman, Anderson, and Nuraliyeva, "The Cost of Corruption in Higher Education," 22.
237 In 2013 there was a high-profile case when a docent of the MGIMO was fired for falsely claiming that he had a Ph.D. diploma from Harvard University (it was done mainly for self-advertisement, this person had a real C.Sc. degree) after being exposed by online Russian media. See: "Iz MGIMO uvolili prisvoivshego garvardskuiu stepen' dotsenta," *Lenta.ru*, 26 February 2013, http://lenta.ru/news/2013/02/26/sudakov/ (as of 14 April 2014).
238 See: Serghei Golunov, *"Malpractices in the Russian Higher Education System: Implications for EU-Russian Education and Science Cooperation"*, EU-Russia Paper 9 (March 2013): 11-12, http://ceurus.ut.ee/wp-content/uploads/2011/06/EU-Russia-Papers-9_Golunov.pdf (as of 14 April 2014).
239 Paso Sahlberg, "The Role of International Organisations in Fighting Education Corruption," in Stephen H. Heyneman (ed.) *Buying your way into Heaven: Education and Corruption in International Perspective* (Rotterdam and Taipei: Sense Publishers, 2009), 150-151.
240 "Standards and Guidelines for Quality Assurance in the European Higher Education Area," *Bologna Process—Higher Education Area* (2005), http://www.ehea.info/Uploads/Documents/Standards-and-Guidelines-for-QA.pdf (as of 5 May 2014).

assurance among its key priorities[241], the struggle with corruption and cheating is not explicitly prioritised: it is revealing that, as of 14 April 2014, the word "corruption" was mentioned just 16 times, the word "cheating" was mentioned just 3 times, and the phrase "academic integrity" was mentioned just 11 times in the European Higher Education Area (EHEA) site's searchable content; in the overwhelming majority of cases these terms were mentioned just either in country reports or in conference proceedings. Thus, while some researchers believe that the EHEA provides mechanisms that to some extent allow corrupted higher education systems and universities to be pressured in to change by the threat of marginalisation[242], I consider these mechanisms rather vague and largely not efficient.

Leading international university ratings, such as the QS World University Rankings and the Times Higher Education World University Rankings, potentially could also serve as a tool through which external actors could prompt Russia to combat educational malpractices more consistently. To achieve high positions for top universities in global rankings is a matter of prestige for Russian authorities: in particular, Russian president Vladimir Putin in 2012 set an objective that five Russian universities should be in the top hundred of the global university rankings by 2020[243]. Unfortunately, as in the case of the Bologna Process, the criteria of such ratings do not clearly take into account corruption and academic integrity issues; thus it is quite possible for universities, allowing a considerable part of their students and researchers to obtain their degrees by fraudulent means, to achieve very high positions in such rankings.

International projects involving universities, departments, groups, and individuals can be affected by reputational considerations or by academic integrity standards that are adhered to by at least one of the participating sides.

---

241 "The Bologna Declaration of 19 June 1999," Bologna Process—Higher Education Area http://www.ehea.info/Uploads/Declarations/BOLOGNA_DECLARATION1.pdf (5 May 2014).

242 Sjur Bergan, "The European Higher Education Area as an Instrument of Transparency?" in Stephen H. Heyneman (ed.) Buying your way into Heaven: Education and Corruption in International Perspective, (Rotterdam and Taipei: Sense Publishers, 2009),131-132.

243 "Putin rasporiadilsya nachat reformy v obrazovanii," Newsland.com, 7 May 2012, http://newsland.com/news/detail/id/952584/ (as of 5 May 2014).

In this case, another side, if interested in cooperation very seriously and not wishing to have this cooperation thwarted, can be prompted to enhance its reputation and to observe academic integrity norms.

This mechanism does not always work though. I have already mentioned in a previous chapter the case when a large Russian university situated in Siberia brought to the UK a team of more than 30 players for a friendly football match. Even some well-known and highly-reputed Western universities invite wealthy and influential Russian officials and politicians with degrees obtained under suspicious circumstances to made presentations or even award some honorary titles to them, especially if honouring such persons could bring funding for university projects.

For instance, the head of one of the most influential Russian corporations who, while holding this full-time position, defended his C.Sc. thesis in 2005 and doctoral thesis already in 2007, according to his theses abstracts[244], was invited to make presentations in the London School of Economics[245], University of Oxford[246], and Harvard University[247] (it should be noted though that in none of these cases was he advertised as a D.Sc.).

In November 2013, the head of an extremely powerful Russian law enforcement agency, invited to participate in a roundtable by the Pantheon-Sorbonne University, was accused of plagiarism by a guest directly during the meeting[248]. It is interesting that this top official for the first time found himself in the midst of such a scandal in 2007[249].

---

244 *Russian State Library*, http://goo.gl/tFyLrp (as of 31 March 2014); *Russian State Library*, http://goo.gl/91ajEl (as of 31 March 2014).
245 "'Russian Railways' as the locomotive of the Russian Economy," *The London School of Economics and Political Science*, http://www.lse.ac.uk/publicEvents/events/2009/20090116t0952z001.aspx (as of 14 April 2014).
246 "Vladimir Yakunin—President of Russian Railways," *Oxford Talks*, 2 February 2012, http://talks.ox.ac.uk/talk/index/7712 (as of 14 April 2014).
247 "Discussion with Vladimir Yakunin, CEO Russian Railways," *Harvard University*, 5 May 2011, http://lists.fas.harvard.edu/pipermail/daviscalendar-list/2011-May/000385.html (as of 14 April 2014).
248 "V Sorbonne studenty obvinili Bastrykina v plagiate," *Lenta.ru*, 20 November 2013, http://top.rbc.ru/incidents/20/11/2013/890074.shtml (as of 14 April 2014).
249 V.N. Chisnikov, "Retsenzia na knigu A.I. Bastrykina 'Znaki ruki. Daktiloskopia'," *Mezhdunarodnaia assotsiatsia sodeistvia pravosudiiu*, 30 May 2011, http://www.iuaj.net/node/746 (as of 14 April 2014).

In May 2014 Ca' Foscari University of Venice conferred honorary fellowship to a Russian minister whose office allegedly funded one of the university's projects. This decision provoked strong protest: more than 200 professors[250] and more than 1000 students of the university signed a petition demanding to cancel the award. Some signatories stressed that this minister was earlier accused of plagiarism[251]. Such a strong protest forced the university authorities to cancel a ceremony scheduled to be held in its premises and this ceremony finally was held in Moscow. A week after the ceremony a prorector of Ca' Foscari University, who actively supported the conferral, had to retire. Finally, the university's Academic Senate, after considering all the pros and cons, confirmed its previous decision to award the fellowship[252], as cancellation of the award could cause a diplomatic scandal. Ironically, on the same day when the session of the Academic Senate was held Dissernet announced that it found illegitimate textual borrowings in this minister's C.Sc. and D.Sc. theses[253].

While well-reputed foreign universities are probably not obliged to investigate closely academic biographies of invited Russian speakers, these cases illustrate both that a tarnished academic personal (and maybe also institutional) reputation in Russia is not necessarily an obstacle for international cooperation even with prestigious partners and that highly influential persons with suspicious academic degrees can easily use top foreign universities for boosting their academic image.

---

250 «Pis'mo 226 professorov i sotrudnikov universiteta Ka' Foskari protiv prisuzhdenia pochëtnogo zvania V. Medinskomu," Polit.ru, 19 May 2014, http://www.polit.ru/article/2014/05/19/226_professors_ca_foscari_letter/ (as of 1 June 2014). In 2012 this minister was accused of making several illegitimate textual borrowings for a synopsis of his thesis. See: "O plagiate v doktorskoi dissertatsii V.R. Medinskogo," Actual'naia istoria, http://actualhistory.ru/medinskyi_plagiat (as of 1 June 2014).
251 "Uvolilas' prorektor Ka' Foskari. Nagradivshaia pochëtnym zvaniem ministra kul'tury RF," Rosbalt, 22 May 2014, http://www.rosbalt.ru/main/2014/05/22/1271046.html (as of 1 June 2014).
252 Pavel Kotliar, "Sorinka Medinskogo v italianskom glazu," Gazeta.ru, 23 May 2014, http://www.gazeta.ru/science/2014/05/23_a_6045513.shtml (as of 1 June 2014).
253 See: "Medinskii Vladimir Rostislavovich," Dissernet.org, http://www.dissernet.org/expertise/medinskivr1997.htm (as of 1 June 2014); Id., http://www.dissernet.org/expertise/medinskyvr1999.htm (as of 1 June 2014); Sergei Parkhomenko, "Delo Medinskogo. Prachechnaia dlia chuzhikh slov," LiveJournal, 23 Мау 2014, Дело Мединского. Прачечная для чужих слов (as of 1 June 2014).

It should also be taken into account that as a result of international sanctions imposed on Russia because of its interference into Ukrainian affairs involving the annexation of Ukrainian territory and because of a self-isolation policy chosen by Moscow in response, Russia could become less sensitive to any international criticism, and its international educational cooperation could be reduced essentially. Still, Russia may be interested in maintaining a good international image for its universities, and thus some chances to prompt it to fight academic malpractice more efficiently will probably remain.

4.5. Conclusion

An efficient approach for combatting corruption and cheating, basing on the best international practices, probably should include an integrated set of measures: not only repercussions but also increasing transparency at all levels of the system, capacity building in personnel, encouraging public activism and university self-governance, and conducting monitoring of reforms, etc. Taking into account the aggressive and highly corrupt environment that surrounds the Russian higher education system, such reforms probably would have only partial success.

Actually, Russian official policy in the field of higher education does not prioritise the struggle with corruption and cheating. While some efforts to combat malpractices are undertaken, such efforts are half-hearted and rely on overcentralisation. Public activists are allowed to provide limited feedback but are not supported when their activities go "too far" by targeting high-standing officials or influential figures in the higher education system. The role of international actors in combatting academic malpractice in Russia is rather low, though it has some potential for increasing if international institutions with Russian participation and some criteria of global university rankings are reformed.

5 CONCLUSIONS

5.1. Roots and relative importance of malpractices

It is not possible to identify a single main reason for the prevalence of malpractice, in comparison to which all other reasons could be considered secondary.

The tiny salaries of ordinary university teachers is a very important factor, as it prompts many teachers to take bribes from students. However, bribery is just one of the numerous kinds of malpractice prevalent in the Russian higher education system, and the prevalence of the majority of the other malpractices can hardly be explained by tiny salaries. Big salaries do not prevent top university managers from taking bribes or from being involved in other financial machinations, as the opportunity to get even more shadow income attracts even well-to-do persons. Taking this into account, there are no grounds to believe that even a sharp increase in salaries of ordinary university teachers could itself dramatically diminish the extent of bribery between teachers and students.

A corrupted and degrading academic culture also matters and it can serve as one of the explanations for the prevalence of a much wider range of malpractices than could be explained by tiny salaries. However, does this mean that just replacing current academics and managers with new not corrupted ones can solve the majority of problems related to corruption and fraud? It is rather doubtful that newly-hired academics and managers, even fully knowing about academic integrity principles, would be able to resist the numerous temptations and pressures deriving from the highly corrupted higher education system and this system's aggressive environment.

Overbureaucratised and a highly authoritarian management system is unfriendly to principled academics, as they sometimes go "too far" in their integrity and do not obey illegitimate informal orders from their bosses. Such a system does not encourage transparency, accountability, university self-governance, and academic and student activism. However, as the Russian experience of the 1990s shows, democratic university management could easily be as corrupt as the authoritarian university management, being dominated by those influence groups that defend their members and oftentimes are reluctant to punish other groups' members to not break the existing balance of power and incur revenge from the other groups. Thus, while over-bureaucratisation and authoritarian management definitely creates ground for corruption and cheating, it is doubtful that removing these factors without taking additional measures (to be considered below) could improve the situation significantly.

Commercialisation of higher education has also created some ground for malpractice as the majority of universities are clearly not interested in expelling those who pay for their studies. However, this is not the only reason for malpractice, as many of them (bribery, embezzlement, clientelism, and dissertation fraud) existed and were relatively widespread in the non-commercialised higher education system of the Soviet Union. Even more important, commercialisation is a key condition for the contemporary Russian higher education system's development, as for the vast majority of universities it would be extremely difficult to exist without it. Thus, the question is rather not in commercialisation itself but in the shape it takes and about its limits: "diploma factories" should be punished or, at least, marginalised, and diplomas should not be given to anyone who pays money for it irrespective of such students' performance.

Massivisation of higher education reduced the quality of control over students' performance, thus creating favourable conditions for cheating. It also made universities more dependent on the total number of students thus (in a similar way to the influence of commercialisation) discouraging such universities from expelling students for bad performance or for resorting to cheating. It should be noted, however, that massivisation is not the main reason for cheating, it is just one of the factors that create the breeding grounds for it.

Finally, the influence of the external environment looks extremely important in some cases. It is much more difficult now than 20 years ago to fight plagiarism and the receiving of unauthorised hints by students because of the Internet and smartphones; however, these and other modern technologies probably could not be abolished for the sake of eliminating educational cheating. Even for a low-corruption Russian university it would be difficult now to resist the pressure of very powerful actors, demanding C.Sc. or D.Sc. diplomas for themselves and high marks for their children, while the untarnished reputation of universities does not have much value in contemporary Russia and is not automatically converted into a massive influx of new entrants. Yet, pressurising and bribe-giving external actors can hardly be blamed for the prevalence of a large part of the malpractices (such as bribery or plagiarism), involving only or predominantly those actors that are internal to the Russian higher education system.

Thus, these and other factors, which create breeding grounds for malpractice, work in combination and therefore targeting just one of these factors would hardly prove to be efficient. It seems that only an approach targeting these factors in combination will have a chance to make an essential difference to the current situation in the Russian higher education system.

5.2. Damage from malpractice

It appears that the most serious kind of damage, caused by some corruption and cheating practices in Russia (e.g. bribery, clientelism, plagiarism, cribbing, and receiving unauthorised hints during exams), is devaluation of higher education and doctoral diplomas. Employing such malpractices it is possible now in Russia to graduate university (even from a formally highly prestigious one) or to defend a doctoral thesis without acquiring any new knowledge or gaining new skills. After this, a graduate who studied just nominally can easily become a manager of some official agency, a lawyer, and in some cases even a doctor, while those who obtained their doctoral degrees by improper means can become top university managers. It is difficult to estimate the scope of this problem on the whole, but when considering current rectors, at least 10% defended their theses under dubious circumstances according to my estimation. If the share of bogus specialists reaches some unknown critical mass, it could probably have catastrophic consequences for the Russian economy, management system, health care, and other spheres.

The second most serious kind of damage, posed by educational malpractices, is degrading academic culture. Probably the vast majority of Russian universities can hardly be considered as bearers of integrity that could be transferred to younger generations. On the contrary, plagiarism and other forms of cheating, sometimes also bribery and clientelism, become normalised in the eyes of many Russian students. Unfortunately, there is not much hope that those graduates, who learnt that corruption and cheating are something normal, could be reliable allies for those authorities who decide to take serious efforts to fight omnipresent corruption, which is now one of the key unsolved problems for the Russian Federation.

The third key consequence of pervasive malpractices in Russian higher education is misallocation of funding and other resources. While ordinary academics receive miserable salaries and many able and conscientious young people cannot enter university, a large part of the funding for higher education and science goes to those unscrupulous students who learn nothing and are not punished for this or to funding of those universities, centres, and groups who undeservedly won competitions only due to connections and bribes.

5.3. Efficiency of counteraction measures

It is amazing that corruption and cheating in Russian higher education are something like an "elephant in the room" for Russian authorities and for managers of the Russian higher education system: everybody knows that the problems are extremely serious but almost nobody gives them primary importance. Instead, the MES and universities prioritise efficiency measured by formal indices, virtually none of which are relevant to the efficiency of a university's anti-corruption and anti-cheating policy. As a result, a university that routinely awards diplomas to those students who systematically cheat and use connections (thus systematically producing fake specialists), turns a blind eye to plagiarised thesis, and is even governed by those who obtained their degrees fraudulently, can easily be considered highly efficient and can be placed at the top of Russian official ratings. While those universities that pursue more principled anti-corruption and anti-cheating policies but fail to meet some formal criteria (e.g. attracting additional funding) can be recognised as inefficient and in the worst case closed.

Nevertheless, it should be noted that the government, the MES, and some universities take some measures to combat malpractices. They have managed to strengthen the control over universities' expenditure and renting policies, to make some sensitive information (e.g. information about incomes of rectors) more transparent, and to take some important steps towards combating corruption and fraud, related to the USE and awarding of doctoral degrees. However, such efforts are half-hearted and largely based on bureaucratic orders of central authorities. Though some limited efforts to get feedback from the academic community are made by the MES, official structures are reluctant to cooperate with informal academic and student activists when they "go too far" and target "too influential" figures.

Academic and student activist movements are hardly able to cover all relevant issues systematically but are able to make valuable contribution to combatting some malpractices and to attracting public attention to the situation in some individual universities. Dissernet, focusing on combatting dissertation fraud, is an especially noteworthy initiative of this kind that uses up-to-date IT and networking technologies and manages to achieve impressive results despite an unfriendly official attitude and resistance from very influential people that have been targeted. Yet, taking into account that a large part of Russian top politicians, officials, and other influential figures within the Russian higher education system itself have "dubious" doctoral degrees and that such figures are the backbone of Russian authoritarianism, it is not clear if Dissernet's activity will prove to be able to achieve the essential cleansing of the academic community from those who committed dissertation fraud.

For the international (primarily the EU's) academic community, corruption and cheating in the Russian higher education system is also something like an elephant in the room. Some Russian universities can be considered as respectable international cooperation partners and can occupy decent positions in global university rankings despite being involved in high-profile scandals concerning corruption and cheating. There are many cases when Russian top university managers participated in joint projects actually doing nothing or going for de facto tourist trips using the cooperation with partner universities as a pretext. Russian top managers, who defended their doctoral theses under very suspicious circumstances and in some cases were publicly accused of plagiarism, are invited to give lectures in top Western universities. While the problem of the prevalence of corruption and cheating in the Russian higher education system is widely known, there are no effective levers to prompt Russia to take more serious efforts to combat malpractice. Unfortunately, such mechanisms, e.g. the Bologna Process, are not effective for combatting educational malpractice in participating countries and universities, while the criteria of leading global international rankings do not prevent highly corrupt universities from taking very high positions in them.

5.4. Recommendations

As the prevalence of malpractice in the Russian higher education system is caused by numerous factors of comparable importance and as some of these factors are external to the system, there is no single measure that could bring decisive success. Instead, a complex of measures, implemented by various actors, is needed. I propose below a set of recommendations for such groups of actors as the governmental agencies and the MES in particular, universities, non-governmental organisations, and foreign actors.

The government and the MES in particular should do their best to increase salaries of ordinary university teachers while decreasing their academic workload. Under the conditions of demographic decline in Russia, it is not necessary to increase funding to achieve these purposes, one rather needs to decrease funding and to cut academic jobs at a slower rate than that at which the number of students reduces. This would be just a restoration of justice since it would restore the academic workload that university teachers had before the disastrous massivisation wave of the 1990s-2000s. Apart from this, the MES should avoid provoking universities, even indirectly, to inflate average students' marks and artificially increase the number of successful doctoral theses' defences. Grants and other competitions organised by the MES should be made as transparent as possible and independent observers (including foreigners) should be welcomed as award panel members and evaluators.

Even more important, the government should reconsider its current centralised and overbureauctised policy in favour of encouraging greater university autonomy and real working self-governance, while diminishing the quasi-autocratic power of rectors and other managers inside their universities. Democratic university governance, including really independent (not "pocket" as usually happens now) trade unions and student unions, looks to be a necessary prerequisite for establishing effective and transparent control over the integrity of the education process and over other spheres of university life. The absence of democratic university governance makes rectorates poorly accountable, while the MES, requiring universities to be efficient, does not have its performance properly assessed by those ordinary representatives of the Russian academic community that often suffer from the ministry's ill-thought and sometimes controversial decisions, some of which (such as "strange" appointments of rectors, non-investigating high-profile dissertation scandals, or dubious non-transparent grant awarding decisions) can be caused by corruption. It is hardly possible to stop the massive production of bogus specialists without empowering and protecting the still numerous principled academics and without student activism.

As the current Russian political regime is authoritarian, the government now looks to be not very interested in democratised university governance, since it can be seen as a challenge to the regime's power. However, the consequences of non-democratisation may be even more bitter, as the massive influx of bogus specialists to positions of responsibility in various spheres could be catastrophic for Russia when under the conditions of tough global competition.

While encouraging democratic university governance looks to be a necessary step in combatting corruption and cheating, it would be hardly sufficient per se without the introduction and proper implementation of anti-corruption and anti-cheating norms, training of staff in such implementation, transparent reporting, promoting academic integrity, stimulating academic mobility (that is very low in Russia now), and making competition for academic positions real instead of imitational. The MES and other governmental agencies probably should not impose all of this on universities directly, but they could help universities by producing recommendations and handbooks, stimulating successful universities by additional funding, and by advancing their positions in official ratings. As in Russia an untarnished reputation cannot be easily converted into an influx of new entrants and inflow of additional money, it seems to be important to encourage universities pursuing principled policies by informational support and in some cases by additional funding, reimbursing such universities for financial loss from expelling unscrupulous students. The MES could play the role of arbiter considering some appeals from those who suffered from unjust decisions at a university level (e.g. from those who were accused of plagiarism erroneously). Finally, the MES could organise the gathering and processing of feedback from ordinary academics in various universities, including an evaluation of the universities' performance in fighting corruption and cheating.

As repeatedly mentioned, the relevant reforms just inside the higher education system can bring just half-hearted results at best. Thus, general reforms of national legislation and improving law enforcement practices may be needed. Among all, improving the article of the Criminal Code concerning plagiarism (and maybe also transferring it to the Administrative Offences Code) is needed: on the one hand, the article should penalise such plagiarism that does not inflict large-scale damage to a rights holder and, on the other hand, should not make using the very word "plagiarism" for substantiated accusations of academics and students punishable. While it can hardly be expected that the current regime will support political democratisation for the sake of diminishing the coercive influence of especially powerful actors, the government could, at least, empower universities, making them more capable to withstand illegal pressure from powerful officials. This can be done by granting representatives of universities the informal right to report such problems to those powerful figures who can really solve them, and also by granting universities stable access to the most influential regional and in some cases to federal media.

While the role of the MES and the government in combatting academic malpractices can be very important, the main job should be done at the level of universities. The latter should have clear and working anti-corruption and anti-cheating policies and ethical codes (information on decisions concerning serious cases of academic integrity violation could be made publicly accessible), to make financial and procurement information more transparent, to train the staff in anti-corruption and anti-cheating control and to educate them in academic integrity, and to defend teachers and students from illicit pressure by those who have more power. Not only the typical measures derived from worldwide experience but also some non-trivial measures could be considered. For instance, taking into account the disastrous pervasiveness of student plagiarism in Russian universities, all student papers could be published online and anyone who manages to find plagiarism could be rewarded at the expense of the author of the plagiarised paper. It is very important, at the same time, to provide students with an opportunity to appeal against accusations of plagiarism that are not sufficiently grounded to some bodies authorised to handle such cases.

While Russian non-governmental organisations and informal academic initiatives dealing with the relevant issues have to work under unfriendly conditions of the authoritarian regime, there is a large field of activities for such organisations and initiatives apart from combatting dissertation fraud and defending university teachers' rights. Academic activists can learn more from a rather popular and successful but yet largely non-academic Russian networking initiative on monitoring public purchases *RosPil*. There is also the need for systematic monitoring of the relevant events that happen in various individual Russian universities and in supporting the informal initiatives launched by adherents of integrity among students. By the way, there are still virtually no efficiently working all-Russian student networks of this kind.

Some foreign and international actors could also make valuable contributions to combatting corruption and cheating in Russia. In particular, the Bologna Process, leading global university rankings, and international university partnerships could be reformed in a way that would prompt Russian and some other countries' universities to take more vigorous efforts when maintaining academic integrity. While it may be difficult to evaluate the level of pervasiveness of corruption and cheating in individual universities, it may be easier to check if anti-corruption and anti-cheating policies exist and if such policies are really implemented (at least transparently), to identify the relevant high-profile plagiarism scandals, and cases of unlawful prosecution of these universities' teachers or students. University ranking agencies could also include questions concerning such policies and the pervasiveness of various malpractices in their expert surveys. It could also be recommended for them to cooperate with such Russian non-governmental initiatives as Dissernet and "*Solidarnost*'" the Trade Union for University Workers, using their information as an additional source for ranking.

Even taken in combination, the proposed measures will not necessary bring decisive success as some of them may not work under Russian conditions and as the perpetrators of malpractices can adapt to changing circumstances. Thus, independent monitoring of the reforms and further research on Russian educational malpractices and on policies directed against them may be needed.

INDEX

academic activism 18-9, 47, 55, 57, 66, 70-1, 73-6, 81, 84-6, 89, 92-102, 108-9, 113, 116-7; see also Dissernet, Society of Scientific Workers, *Solidarnost'* (The Interregional Trade Union of University Workers), *Troitskii variant*

academic integrity: degradation of 15, 39, 109, 112; promotion of 85, 103, 115
academic tourism 59-60, 102, 114
academic workload 32-3, 92, 102, 114
authoritarian university management, *see* rectors
authoritarian political regime, the influence of: 41-4, 46, 79, 113, 115, 117
Bologna Process 103-4, 114, 117
bribery: 15, 17, 49, 51-2, 54, 78, 90-1, 109-12; legal treatment of 17, 61, 82, 86; of top managers 44, 54, 61, of ordinary teachers 16, 41, 44-6, 57, 61-3, 65, 93, 109; prevalence of 62-3; the role of intermediaries in 61-2
Bureaucratisation 18, 20, 28, 35-6, 39, 78, 80, 84, 86, 89, 92, 95, 109-10, 113
capacity building of personnel 85, 107
cheating: definition of 51-2, 63, 66; *see also* cribbing, ghost writing, plagiarism, receiving unauthorised hints
corruption, definition of 15, 50-2
commercialisation of higher education 20, 23, 28, 33-4, 46, 110
cribbing 15, 29, 46, 65, 66-8, 77, 79, 111
Council of Science under the MES 90
Moscow State Pegagogical University

clientelism: 15-6, 32-3, 36, 38, 40, 54, 56, 59-60, 63, 77, 79, 110-2; *see also* nepotism
Dissernet 18, 96, 102, 106, 113, 118
dissertation fraud ; 19-20, 55-7, 70, 75-6, 81, 86-9, 95, 110, 115, 117; *see also* plagiarism
embezzlement 15, 36, 52, 59, 78, 82, 102, 110
ethical code 51, 83-4, 91-2, 117
European University in St Petersburg 42, 91
extortion 51-2, 62-3, 86, 90
Gel'fand, M. 89, 97
ghost writing 63, 66, 69-70, 77-8
Hallak, J. 52, 82, 84
Heyneman, S. 17, 102
Higher School of Economics (HSE) 62, 90, 91
IT environment, influence of 45-7, 113
Khanin, G. 29-31
laying universities 58-9
Leibovich, O. 17, 31, 39, 41, 45
Leontieva, E. 17, 44, 50
List of the VAK 27, 87-8
Livanov, D. 74-5, 87, 90, 95, 99
massivisation of higher education 18, 28-34, 46, 80, 110, 114
Ministry of Education and Science (MES) 24, 26, 31-2, 35, 37-8, 41-2, 46, 48, 53-7, 65-6, 73-5, 80, 86-90, 95, 97-100, 112-116
Moscow State Institute of International Relations (MGIMO) 91, 102
Shamkhalov, F. 57

(MSPU) 75, 88, 89
Nepotism 42, 44-5, 59, 62, 89
OD Group 93-4
Olympiads for schoolchildren 53, 63, 65-6
Parkhomenko, S. 96, 98, 101
Pirogov Russian National Research Medical University 64, 91
plagiarism 15, 17-20, 36, 45-6, 49, 66, 68-70, 75-6, 78-9, 86, 88-90, 92-4, 96-101, 105-6, 110-2, 114, 118; by students 16, 32, 36, 67-8, 77, 116-7; in social sciences 70; in "nonhumanitarian" sciences 70-1; see also dissertation fraud
Poisson, M. 52, 84
procurement fraud 17-8, 58, 77, 83, 94
Public Council (under the MES) 90
Putin, V. 71, 104
Russian Presidential Academy of National Economy and Public Administration (RANEPA) 25, 75
rector's list 63
rectors: and authoritarian management 36-7, 42, 54, 58, 60-1, 63-4, 100, 115; and higher authorities 37-9, 43-4, 53-6, 73, 86; election and appointment procedures 26, 37-8; incomes of 30, 87, 113
Rosobrnadzor 24, 43, 64, 67, 87
Rostovtsev, A. 75, 96, 98-9; "thesis mincer" of 75, 96
salaries: of ordinary university teachers 37, 39, 40-1, 45, 78, 87, 92, 102, 109, 112, 114; of rectors, see rectors, incomes of
selection of elites 77

Shushkova, N. 17, 31, 39, 41, 45
Society of Scientific Workers 101
Solidarnost' (The Interregional Trade Union of University Workers) 101, 118
Solzhenitsyn, A. 29
St Petersburg State University (SPSU) 86, 91
student activism 93-4, 109, 113, 115; see also OD Group
Troitskii variant (newspaper) 18, 94-6
unauthorised hints during exams 15, 66-8, 77, 83, 86, 90-1, 110-11
university rankings 21,104, 108, 112-4, 116-8
USE (Unified State Exam) 24, 27, 53, 58, 63-7, 76-7, 87, 89, 90, 95, 113
VAK (Higher Attestation Commission) 24-27, 56-7, 69-70, 75-6, 87-90, 97-100
Zaiakin, A. 95
Zimin, D. 94, 96
Žižek, S. 40

SOVIET AND POST-SOVIET POLITICS AND SOCIETY

Edited by Dr. Andreas Umland

ISSN 1614-3515

1   Андреас Умланд (ред.)
    Воплощение Европейской
    конвенции по правам человека в
    России
    Философские, юридические и
    эмпирические исследования
    ISBN 3-89821-387-0

2   Christian Wipperfürth
    Russland – ein vertrauenswürdiger
    Partner?
    Grundlagen, Hintergründe und Praxis
    gegenwärtiger russischer Außenpolitik
    Mit einem Vorwort von Heinz Timmermann
    ISBN 3-89821-401-X

3   Manja Hussner
    Die Übernahme internationalen Rechts
    in die russische und deutsche
    Rechtsordnung
    Eine vergleichende Analyse zur
    Völkerrechtsfreundlichkeit der Verfassungen
    der Russländischen Föderation und der
    Bundesrepublik Deutschland
    Mit einem Vorwort von Rainer Arnold
    ISBN 3-89821-438-9

4   Matthew Tejada
    Bulgaria's Democratic Consolidation
    and the Kozloduy Nuclear Power Plant
    (KNPP)
    The Unattainability of Closure
    With a foreword by Richard J. Crampton
    ISBN 3-89821-439-7

5   Марк Григорьевич Меерович
    Квадратные метры, определяющие
    сознание
    Государственная жилищная политика в
    СССР. 1921 – 1941 гг
    ISBN 3-89821-474-5

6   Andrei P. Tsygankov, Pavel
    A.Tsygankov (Eds.)
    New Directions in Russian
    International Studies
    ISBN 3-89821-422-2

7   Марк Григорьевич Меерович
    Как власть народ к труду приучала
    Жилище в СССР – средство управления
    людьми. 1917 – 1941 гг.
    С предисловием Елены Осокиной
    ISBN 3-89821-495-8

8   David J. Galbreath
    Nation-Building and Minority Politics
    in Post-Socialist States
    Interests, Influence and Identities in Estonia
    and Latvia
    With a foreword by David J. Smith
    ISBN 3-89821-467-2

9   Алексей Юрьевич Безугольный
    Народы Кавказа в Вооруженных
    силах СССР в годы Великой
    Отечественной войны 1941-1945 гг.
    С предисловием Николая Бугая
    ISBN 3-89821-475-3

10 Вячеслав Лихачев и Владимир
    Прибыловский (ред.)
    Русское Национальное Единство,
    1990-2000. В 2-х томах
    ISBN 3-89821-523-7

11 Николай Бугай (ред.)
    Народы стран Балтии в условиях
    сталинизма (1940-е – 1950-е годы)
    Документированная история
    ISBN 3-89821-525-3

12 Ingmar Bredies (Hrsg.)
    Zur Anatomie der Orange Revolution
    in der Ukraine
    Wechsel des Elitenregimes oder Triumph des
    Parlamentarismus?
    ISBN 3-89821-524-5

13 Anastasia V. Mitrofanova
    The Politicization of Russian
    Orthodoxy
    Actors and Ideas
    With a foreword by William C. Gay
    ISBN 3-89821-481-8

14 *Nathan D. Larson*
Alexander Solzhenitsyn and the
Russo-Jewish Question
ISBN 3-89821-483-4

15 *Guido Houben*
Kulturpolitik und Ethnizität
Staatliche Kunstförderung im Russland der neunziger Jahre
Mit einem Vorwort von Gert Weisskirchen
ISBN 3-89821-542-3

16 *Leonid Luks*
Der russische „Sonderweg"?
Aufsätze zur neuesten Geschichte Russlands im europäischen Kontext
ISBN 3-89821-496-6

17 *Евгений Мороз*
История «Мёртвой воды» – от страшной сказки к большой политике
Политическое неоязычество в постсоветской России
ISBN 3-89821-551-2

18 *Александр Верховский и Галина Кожевникова (ред.)*
Этническая и религиозная интолерантность в российских СМИ
Результаты мониторинга 2001-2004 гг.
ISBN 3-89821-569-5

19 *Christian Ganzer*
Sowjetisches Erbe und ukrainische Nation
Das Museum der Geschichte des Zaporoger Kosakentums auf der Insel Chortycja
Mit einem Vorwort von Frank Golczewski
ISBN 3-89821-504-0

20 *Эльза-Баир Гучинова*
Помнить нельзя забыть
Антропология депортационной травмы калмыков
С предисловием Кэролайн Хамфри
ISBN 3-89821-506-7

21 *Юлия Лидерман*
Мотивы «проверки» и «испытания» в постсоветской культуре
Советское прошлое в российском кинематографе 1990-х годов
С предисловием Евгения Марголита
ISBN 3-89821-511-3

22 *Tanya Lokshina, Ray Thomas, Mary Mayer (Eds.)*
The Imposition of a Fake Political Settlement in the Northern Caucasus
The 2003 Chechen Presidential Election
ISBN 3-89821-436-2

23 *Timothy McCajor Hall, Rosie Read (Eds.)*
Changes in the Heart of Europe
Recent Ethnographies of Czechs, Slovaks, Roma, and Sorbs
With an afterword by Zdeněk Salzmann
ISBN 3-89821-606-3

24 *Christian Autengruber*
Die politischen Parteien in Bulgarien und Rumänien
Eine vergleichende Analyse seit Beginn der 90er Jahre
Mit einem Vorwort von Dorothée de Nève
ISBN 3-89821-476-1

25 *Annette Freyberg-Inan with Radu Cristescu*
The Ghosts in Our Classrooms, or: John Dewey Meets Ceauşescu
The Promise and the Failures of Civic Education in Romania
ISBN 3-89821-416-8

26 *John B. Dunlop*
The 2002 Dubrovka and 2004 Beslan Hostage Crises
A Critique of Russian Counter-Terrorism
With a foreword by Donald N. Jensen
ISBN 3-89821-608-X

27 *Peter Koller*
Das touristische Potenzial von Kam''janec–Podil's'kyj
Eine fremdenverkehrsgeographische Untersuchung der Zukunftsperspektiven und Maßnahmenplanung zur Destinationsentwicklung des „ukrainischen Rothenburg"
Mit einem Vorwort von Kristiane Klemm
ISBN 3-89821-640-3

28 *Françoise Daucé, Elisabeth Sieca-Kozlowski (Eds.)*
Dedovshchina in the Post-Soviet Military
Hazing of Russian Army Conscripts in a Comparative Perspective
With a foreword by Dale Herspring
ISBN 3-89821-616-0

29 Florian Strasser
    Zivilgesellschaftliche Einflüsse auf die
    Orange Revolution
    Die gewaltlose Massenbewegung und die
    ukrainische Wahlkrise 2004
    Mit einem Vorwort von Egbert Jahn
    ISBN 3-89821-648-9

30 Rebecca S. Katz
    The Georgian Regime Crisis of 2003-
    2004
    A Case Study in Post-Soviet Media
    Representation of Politics, Crime and
    Corruption
    ISBN 3-89821-413-3

31 Vladimir Kantor
    Willkür oder Freiheit
    Beiträge zur russischen Geschichtsphilosophie
    Ediert von Dagmar Herrmann sowie mit
    einem Vorwort versehen von Leonid Luks
    ISBN 3-89821-589-X

32 Laura A. Victoir
    The Russian Land Estate Today
    A Case Study of Cultural Politics in Post-
    Soviet Russia
    With a foreword by Priscilla Roosevelt
    ISBN 3-89821-426-5

33 Ivan Katchanovski
    Cleft Countries
    Regional Political Divisions and Cultures in
    Post-Soviet Ukraine and Moldova
    With a foreword by Francis Fukuyama
    ISBN 3-89821-558-X

34 Florian Mühlfried
    Postsowjetische Feiern
    Das Georgische Bankett im Wandel
    Mit einem Vorwort von Kevin Tuite
    ISBN 3-89821-601-2

35 Roger Griffin, Werner Loh, Andreas
    Umland (Eds.)
    Fascism Past and Present, West and
    East
    An International Debate on Concepts and
    Cases in the Comparative Study of the
    Extreme Right
    With an afterword by Walter Laqueur
    ISBN 3-89821-674-8

36 Sebastian Schlegel
    Der „Weiße Archipel"
    Sowjetische Atomstädte 1945-1991
    Mit einem Geleitwort von Thomas Bohn
    ISBN 3-89821-679-9

37 Vyacheslav Likhachev
    Political Anti-Semitism in Post-Soviet
    Russia
    Actors and Ideas in 1991-2003
    Edited and translated from Russian by Eugene
    Veklerov
    ISBN 3-89821-529-6

38 Josette Baer (Ed.)
    Preparing Liberty in Central Europe
    Political Texts from the Spring of Nations
    1848 to the Spring of Prague 1968
    With a foreword by Zdeněk V. David
    ISBN 3-89821-546-6

39 Михаил Лукьянов
    Российский консерватизм и
    реформа, 1907-1914
    С предисловием Марка Д. Стейнберга
    ISBN 3-89821-503-2

40 Nicola Melloni
    Market Without Economy
    The 1998 Russian Financial Crisis
    With a foreword by Eiji Furukawa
    ISBN 3-89821-407-9

41 Dmitrij Chmelnizki
    Die Architektur Stalins
    Bd. 1: Studien zu Ideologie und Stil
    Bd. 2: Bilddokumentation
    Mit einem Vorwort von Bruno Flierl
    ISBN 3-89821-515-6

42 Katja Yafimava
    Post-Soviet Russian-Belarusian
    Relationships
    The Role of Gas Transit Pipelines
    With a foreword by Jonathan P. Stern
    ISBN 3-89821-655-1

43 Boris Chavkin
    Verflechtungen der deutschen und
    russischen Zeitgeschichte
    Aufsätze und Archivfunde zu den
    Beziehungen Deutschlands und der
    Sowjetunion von 1917 bis 1991
    Ediert von Markus Edlinger sowie mit einem
    Vorwort versehen von Leonid Luks
    ISBN 3-89821-756-6

44 *Anastasija Grynenko in Zusammenarbeit mit Claudia Dathe*
Die Terminologie des Gerichtswesens der Ukraine und Deutschlands im Vergleich
Eine übersetzungswissenschaftliche Analyse juristischer Fachbegriffe im Deutschen, Ukrainischen und Russischen
Mit einem Vorwort von Ulrich Hartmann
ISBN 3-89821-691-8

45 *Anton Burkov*
The Impact of the European Convention on Human Rights on Russian Law
Legislation and Application in 1996-2006
With a foreword by Françoise Hampson
ISBN 978-3-89821-639-5

46 *Stina Torjesen, Indra Overland (Eds.)*
International Election Observers in Post-Soviet Azerbaijan
Geopolitical Pawns or Agents of Change?
ISBN 978-3-89821-743-9

47 *Taras Kuzio*
Ukraine – Crimea – Russia
Triangle of Conflict
ISBN 978-3-89821-761-3

48 *Claudia Šabič*
"Ich erinnere mich nicht, aber L'viv!"
Zur Funktion kultureller Faktoren für die Institutionalisierung und Entwicklung einer ukrainischen Region
Mit einem Vorwort von Melanie Tatur
ISBN 978-3-89821-752-1

49 *Marlies Bilz*
Tatarstan in der Transformation
Nationaler Diskurs und Politische Praxis 1988-1994
Mit einem Vorwort von Frank Golczewski
ISBN 978-3-89821-722-4

50 *Марлен Ларюэль (ред.)*
Современные интерпретации русского национализма
ISBN 978-3-89821-795-8

51 *Sonja Schüler*
Die ethnische Dimension der Armut
Roma im postsozialistischen Rumänien
Mit einem Vorwort von Anton Sterbling
ISBN 978-3-89821-776-7

52 *Галина Кожевникова*
Радикальный национализм в России и противодействие ему
Сборник докладов Центра «Сова» за 2004-2007 гг.
С предисловием Александра Верховского
ISBN 978-3-89821-721-7

53 *Галина Кожевникова и Владимир Прибыловский*
Российская власть в биографиях I
Высшие должностные лица РФ в 2004 г.
ISBN 978-3-89821-796-5

54 *Галина Кожевникова и Владимир Прибыловский*
Российская власть в биографиях II
Члены Правительства РФ в 2004 г.
ISBN 978-3-89821-797-2

55 *Галина Кожевникова и Владимир Прибыловский*
Российская власть в биографиях III
Руководители федеральных служб и агентств РФ в 2004 г.
ISBN 978-3-89821-798-9

56 *Ileana Petroniu*
Privatisierung in Transformationsökonomien
Determinanten der Restrukturierungs-Bereitschaft am Beispiel Polens, Rumäniens und der Ukraine
Mit einem Vorwort von Rainer W. Schäfer
ISBN 978-3-89821-790-3

57 *Christian Wipperfürth*
Russland und seine GUS-Nachbarn
Hintergründe, aktuelle Entwicklungen und Konflikte in einer ressourcenreichen Region
ISBN 978-3-89821-801-6

58 *Togzhan Kassenova*
From Antagonism to Partnership
The Uneasy Path of the U.S.-Russian Cooperative Threat Reduction
With a foreword by Christoph Bluth
ISBN 978-3-89821-707-1

59 *Alexander Höllwerth*
Das sakrale eurasische Imperium des Aleksandr Dugin
Eine Diskursanalyse zum postsowjetischen russischen Rechtsextremismus
Mit einem Vorwort von Dirk Uffelmann
ISBN 978-3-89821-813-9

60   *Олег Рябов*
«Россия-Матушка»
Национализм, гендер и война в России XX века
С предисловием Елены Гощило
ISBN 978-3-89821-487-2

61   *Ivan Maistrenko*
Borot'bism
A Chapter in the History of the Ukrainian Revolution
With a new introduction by Chris Ford
Translated by George S. N. Luckyj with the assistance of Ivan L. Rudnytsky
ISBN 978-3-89821-697-5

62   *Maryna Romanets*
Anamorphosic Texts and Reconfigured Visions
Improvised Traditions in Contemporary Ukrainian and Irish Literature
ISBN 978-3-89821-576-3

63   *Paul D'Anieri and Taras Kuzio (Eds.)*
Aspects of the Orange Revolution I
Democratization and Elections in Post-Communist Ukraine
ISBN 978-3-89821-698-2

64   *Bohdan Harasymiw in collaboration with Oleh S. Ilnytzkyj (Eds.)*
Aspects of the Orange Revolution II
Information and Manipulation Strategies in the 2004 Ukrainian Presidential Elections
ISBN 978-3-89821-699-9

65   *Ingmar Bredies, Andreas Umland and Valentin Yakushik (Eds.)*
Aspects of the Orange Revolution III
The Context and Dynamics of the 2004 Ukrainian Presidential Elections
ISBN 978-3-89821-803-0

66   *Ingmar Bredies, Andreas Umland and Valentin Yakushik (Eds.)*
Aspects of the Orange Revolution IV
Foreign Assistance and Civic Action in the 2004 Ukrainian Presidential Elections
ISBN 978-3-89821-808-5

67   *Ingmar Bredies, Andreas Umland and Valentin Yakushik (Eds.)*
Aspects of the Orange Revolution V
Institutional Observation Reports on the 2004 Ukrainian Presidential Elections
ISBN 978-3-89821-809-2

68   *Taras Kuzio (Ed.)*
Aspects of the Orange Revolution VI
Post-Communist Democratic Revolutions in Comparative Perspective
ISBN 978-3-89821-820-7

69   *Tim Bohse*
Autoritarismus statt Selbstverwaltung
Die Transformation der kommunalen Politik in der Stadt Kaliningrad 1990-2005
Mit einem Geleitwort von Stefan Troebst
ISBN 978-3-89821-782-8

70   *David Rupp*
Die Rußländische Föderation und die russischsprachige Minderheit in Lettland
Eine Fallstudie zur Anwaltspolitik Moskaus gegenüber den russophonen Minderheiten im „Nahen Ausland" von 1991 bis 2002
Mit einem Vorwort von Helmut Wagner
ISBN 978-3-89821-778-1

71   *Taras Kuzio*
Theoretical and Comparative Perspectives on Nationalism
New Directions in Cross-Cultural and Post-Communist Studies
With a foreword by Paul Robert Magocsi
ISBN 978-3-89821-815-3

72   *Christine Teichmann*
Die Hochschultransformation im heutigen Osteuropa
Kontinuität und Wandel bei der Entwicklung des postkommunistischen Universitätswesens
Mit einem Vorwort von Oskar Anweiler
ISBN 978-3-89821-842-9

73   *Julia Kusznir*
Der politische Einfluss von Wirtschaftseliten in russischen Regionen
Eine Analyse am Beispiel der Erdöl- und Erdgasindustrie, 1992-2005
Mit einem Vorwort von Wolfgang Eichwede
ISBN 978-3-89821-821-4

74   *Alena Vysotskaya*
Russland, Belarus und die EU-Osterweiterung
Zur Minderheitenfrage und zum Problem der Freizügigkeit des Personenverkehrs
Mit einem Vorwort von Katlijn Malfliet
ISBN 978-3-89821-822-1

75 *Heiko Pleines (Hrsg.)*
Corporate Governance in postsozialistischen Volkswirtschaften
ISBN 978-3-89821-766-8

76 *Stefan Ihrig*
Wer sind die Moldawier?
Rumänismus versus Moldowanismus in Historiographie und Schulbüchern der Republik Moldova, 1991-2006
Mit einem Vorwort von Holm Sundhaussen
ISBN 978-3-89821-466-7

77 *Galina Kozhevnikova in collaboration with Alexander Verkhovsky and Eugene Veklerov*
Ultra-Nationalism and Hate Crimes in Contemporary Russia
The 2004-2006 Annual Reports of Moscow's SOVA Center
With a foreword by Stephen D. Shenfield
ISBN 978-3-89821-868-9

78 *Florian Küchler*
The Role of the European Union in Moldova's Transnistria Conflict
With a foreword by Christopher Hill
ISBN 978-3-89821-850-4

79 *Bernd Rechel*
The Long Way Back to Europe
Minority Protection in Bulgaria
With a foreword by Richard Crampton
ISBN 978-3-89821-863-4

80 *Peter W. Rodgers*
Nation, Region and History in Post-Communist Transitions
Identity Politics in Ukraine, 1991-2006
With a foreword by Vera Tolz
ISBN 978-3-89821-903-7

81 *Stephanie Solywoda*
The Life and Work of Semen L. Frank
A Study of Russian Religious Philosophy
With a foreword by Philip Walters
ISBN 978-3-89821-457-5

82 *Vera Sokolova*
Cultural Politics of Ethnicity
Discourses on Roma in Communist Czechoslovakia
ISBN 978-3-89821-864-1

83 *Natalya Shevchik Ketenci*
Kazakhstani Enterprises in Transition
The Role of Historical Regional Development in Kazakhstan's Post-Soviet Economic Transformation
ISBN 978-3-89821-831-3

84 *Martin Malek, Anna Schor-Tschudnowskaja (Hrsg.)*
Europa im Tschetschenienkrieg
Zwischen politischer Ohnmacht und Gleichgültigkeit
Mit einem Vorwort von Lipchan Basajewa
ISBN 978-3-89821-676-0

85 *Stefan Meister*
Das postsowjetische Universitätswesen zwischen nationalem und internationalem Wandel
Die Entwicklung der regionalen Hochschule in Russland als Gradmesser der Systemtransformation
Mit einem Vorwort von Joan DeBardeleben
ISBN 978-3-89821-891-7

86 *Konstantin Sheiko in collaboration with Stephen Brown*
Nationalist Imaginings of the Russian Past
Anatolii Fomenko and the Rise of Alternative History in Post-Communist Russia
With a foreword by Donald Ostrowski
ISBN 978-3-89821-915-0

87 *Sabine Jenni*
Wie stark ist das „Einige Russland"?
Zur Parteibindung der Eliten und zum Wahlerfolg der Machtpartei
im Dezember 2007
Mit einem Vorwort von Klaus Armingeon
ISBN 978-3-89821-961-7

88 *Thomas Borén*
Meeting-Places of Transformation
Urban Identity, Spatial Representations and Local Politics in Post-Soviet St Petersburg
ISBN 978-3-89821-739-2

89 *Aygul Ashirova*
Stalinismus und Stalin-Kult in Zentralasien
Turkmenistan 1924-1953
Mit einem Vorwort von Leonid Luks
ISBN 978-3-89821-987-7

90 Leonid Luks
    Freiheit oder imperiale Größe?
    Essays zu einem russischen Dilemma
    ISBN 978-3-8382-0011-8

91 Christopher Gilley
    The 'Change of Signposts' in the
    Ukrainian Emigration
    A Contribution to the History of
    Sovietophilism in the 1920s
    With a foreword by Frank Golczewski
    ISBN 978-3-89821-965-5

92 Philipp Casula, Jeronim Perovic
    (Eds.)
    Identities and Politics
    During the Putin Presidency
    The Discursive Foundations of Russia's
    Stability
    With a foreword by Heiko Haumann
    ISBN 978-3-8382-0015-6

93 Marcel Viëtor
    Europa und die Frage
    nach seinen Grenzen im Osten
    Zur Konstruktion ‚europäischer Identität' in
    Geschichte und Gegenwart
    Mit einem Vorwort von Albrecht Lehmann
    ISBN 978-3-8382-0045-3

94 Ben Hellman, Andrei Rogachevskii
    Filming the Unfilmable
    Casper Wrede's 'One Day in the Life
    of Ivan Denisovich'
    Second, Revised and Expanded Edition
    ISBN 978-3-8382-0044-6

95 Eva Fuchslocher
    Vaterland, Sprache, Glaube
    Orthodoxie und Nationenbildung
    am Beispiel Georgiens
    Mit einem Vorwort von Christina von Braun
    ISBN 978-3-89821-884-9

96 Vladimir Kantor
    Das Westlertum und der Weg
    Russlands
    Zur Entwicklung der russischen Literatur und
    Philosophie
    Ediert von Dagmar Herrmann
    Mit einem Beitrag von Nikolaus Lobkowicz
    ISBN 978-3-8382-0102-3

97 Kamran Musayev
    Die postsowjetische Transformation
    im Baltikum und Südkaukasus
    Eine vergleichende Untersuchung der
    politischen Entwicklung Lettlands und
    Aserbaidschans 1985-2009
    Mit einem Vorwort von Leonid Luks
    Ediert von Sandro Henschel
    ISBN 978-3-8382-0103-0

98 Tatiana Zhurzhenko
    Borderlands into Bordered Lands
    Geopolitics of Identity in Post-Soviet Ukraine
    With a foreword by Dieter Segert
    ISBN 978-3-8382-0042-2

99 Кирилл Галушко, Лидия Смола
    (ред.)
    Пределы падения – варианты
    украинского будущего
    Аналитико-прогностические исследования
    ISBN 978-3-8382-0148-1

100 Michael Minkenberg (ed.)
    Historical Legacies and the Radical
    Right in Post-Cold War Central and
    Eastern Europe
    With an afterword by Sabrina P. Ramet
    ISBN 978-3-8382-0124-5

101 David-Emil Wickström
    Rocking St. Petersburg
    Transcultural Flows and Identity Politics in
    the St. Petersburg Popular Music Scene
    With a foreword by Yngvar B. Steinholt
    Second, Revised and Expanded Edition
    ISBN 978-3-8382-0100-9

102 Eva Zabka
    Eine neue „Zeit der Wirren"?
    Der spät- und postsowjetische Systemwandel
    1985-2000 im Spiegel russischer
    gesellschaftspolitischer Diskurse
    Mit einem Vorwort von Margareta Mommsen
    ISBN 978-3-8382-0161-0

103 Ulrike Ziemer
    Ethnic Belonging, Gender and
    Cultural Practices
    Youth Identitites in Contemporary Russia
    With a foreword by Anoop Nayak
    ISBN 978-3-8382-0152-8

104   Ksenia Chepikova
      ‚Einiges Russland' - eine zweite
      KPdSU?
      Aspekte der Identitätskonstruktion einer
      postsowjetischen „Partei der Macht"
      Mit einem Vorwort von Torsten Oppelland
      ISBN 978-3-8382-0311-9

105   Леонид Люкс
      Западничество или евразийство?
      Демократия или идеократия?
      Сборник статей об исторических дилеммах
      России
      С предисловием Владимира Кантора
      ISBN 978-3-8382-0211-2

106   Anna Dost
      Das russische Verfassungsrecht auf dem
      Weg zum Föderalismus und zurück
      Zum Konflikt von Rechtsnormen und
      -wirklichkeit in der Russländischen
      Föderation von 1991 bis 2009
      Mit einem Vorwort von Alexander Blankenagel
      ISBN 978-3-8382-0292-1

107   Philipp Herzog
      Sozialistische Völkerfreundschaft,
      nationaler Widerstand oder harmloser
      Zeitvertreib?
      Zur politischen Funktion der Volkskunst
      im sowjetischen Estland
      Mit einem Vorwort von Andreas Kappeler
      ISBN 978-3-8382-0216-7

108   Marlène Laruelle (ed.)
      Russian Nationalism, Foreign Policy,
      and Identity Debates in Putin's Russia
      New Ideological Patterns after the Orange
      Revolution
      ISBN 978-3-8382-0325-6

109   Michail Logvinov
      Russlands Kampf gegen den
      internationalen Terrorismus
      Eine kritische Bestandsaufnahme des
      Bekämpfungsansatzes
      Mit einem Geleitwort von
      Hans-Henning Schröder
      und einem Vorwort von Eckhard Jesse
      ISBN 978-3-8382-0329-4

110   John B. Dunlop
      The Moscow Bombings
      of September 1999
      Examinations of Russian Terrorist Attacks
      at the Onset of Vladimir Putin's Rule
      Second, Revised and Expanded Edition
      ISBN 978-3-8382-0388-1

111   Андрей А. Ковалёв
      Свидетельство из-за кулис
      российской политики I
      Можно ли делать добро из зла?
      (Воспоминания и размышления о
      последних советских и первых
      послесоветских годах)
      With a foreword by Peter Reddaway
      ISBN 978-3-8382-0302-7

112   Андрей А. Ковалёв
      Свидетельство из-за кулис
      российской политики II
      Угроза для себя и окружающих
      (Наблюдения и предостережения
      относительно происходящего после 2000 г.)
      ISBN 978-3-8382-0303-4

113   Bernd Kappenberg
      Zeichen setzen für Europa
      Der Gebrauch europäischer lateinischer
      Sonderzeichen in der deutschen Öffentlichkeit
      Mit einem Vorwort von Peter Schlobinski
      ISBN 978-3-89821-749-1

114   Ivo Mijnssen
      The Quest for an Ideal Youth in
      Putin's Russia I
      Back to Our Future! History, Modernity, and
      Patriotism according to Nashi, 2005-2013
      With a foreword by Jeronim Perović
      Second, Revised and Expanded Edition
      ISBN 978-3-8382-0368-3

115   Jussi Lassila
      The Quest for an Ideal Youth in
      Putin's Russia II
      The Search for Distinctive Conformism in the
      Political Communication of Nashi, 2005-2009
      With a foreword by Kirill Postoutenko
      Second, Revised and Expanded Edition
      ISBN 978-3-8382-0415-4

116   Valerio Trabandt
      Neue Nachbarn, gute Nachbarschaft?
      Die EU als internationaler Akteur am Beispiel
      ihrer Demokratieförderung in Belarus und der
      Ukraine 2004-2009
      Mit einem Vorwort von Jutta Joachim
      ISBN 978-3-8382-0437-6

117 Fabian Pfeiffer
Estlands Außen- und Sicherheitspolitik I
Der estnische Atlantizismus nach der
wiedererlangten Unabhängigkeit 1991-2004
Mit einem Vorwort von Helmut Hubel
ISBN 978-3-8382-0127-6

118 Jana Podßuweit
Estlands Außen- und Sicherheitspolitik II
Handlungsoptionen eines Kleinstaates im
Rahmen seiner EU-Mitgliedschaft (2004-2008)
Mit einem Vorwort von Helmut Hubel
ISBN 978-3-8382-0440-6

119 Karin Pointner
Estlands Außen- und Sicherheitspolitik III
Eine gedächtnispolitische Analyse estnischer
Entwicklungskooperation 2006-2010
Mit einem Vorwort von Karin Liebhart
ISBN 978-3-8382-0435-2

120 Ruslana Vovk
Die Offenheit der ukrainischen
Verfassung für das Völkerrecht und
die europäische Integration
Mit einem Vorwort von Alexander
Blankenagel
ISBN 978-3-8382-0481-9

121 Mykhaylo Banakh
Die Relevanz der Zivilgesellschaft
bei den postkommunistischen
Transformationsprozessen in mittel-
und osteuropäischen Ländern
Das Beispiel der spät- und postsowjetischen
Ukraine 1986-2009
Mit einem Vorwort von Gerhard Simon
ISBN 978-3-8382-0499-4

122 Michael Moser
Language Policy and the Discourse on
Languages in Ukraine under President
Viktor Yanukovych (25 February
2010–28 October 2012)
ISBN 978-3-8382-0497-0 (Paperback edition)
ISBN 978-3-8382-0507-6 (Hardcover edition)

123 Nicole Krome
Russischer Netzwerkkapitalismus
Restrukturierungsprozesse in der
Russischen Föderation am Beispiel des
Luftfahrtunternehmens "Aviastar"
Mit einem Vorwort von Petra Stykow
ISBN 978-3-8382-0534-2

124 David R. Marples
'Our Glorious Past'
Lukashenka's Belarus and
the Great Patriotic War
ISBN 978-3-8382-0574-8 (Paperback edition)
ISBN 978-3-8382-0675-2 (Hardcover edition)

125 Ulf Walther
Russlands "neuer Adel"
Die Macht des Geheimdienstes von
Gorbatschow bis Putin
Mit einem Vorwort von Hans-Georg Wieck
ISBN 978-3-8382-0584-7

126 Simon Geissbühler (Hrsg.)
Kiew – Revolution 3.0
Der Euromaidan 2013/14 und die
Zukunftsperspektiven der Ukraine
ISBN 978-3-8382-0581-6 (Paperback edition)
ISBN 978-3-8382-0681-3 (Hardcover edition)

127 Andrey Makarychev
Russia and the EU
in a Multipolar World
Discourses, Identities, Norms
With a foreword by Klaus Segbers
ISBN 978-3-8382-0629-5

128 Roland Scharff
Kasachstan als postsowjetischer
Wohlfahrtsstaat
Die Transformation des sozialen
Schutzsystems
Mit einem Vorwort von Joachim Ahrens
ISBN 978-3-8382-0622-6

129 Katja Grupp
Bild Lücke Deutschland
Kaliningrader Studierende sprechen über
Deutschland
Mit einem Vorwort von Martin Schulz
ISBN 978-3-8382-0552-6

130 Konstantin Sheiko, Stephen Brown
History as Therapy
Alternative History and Nationalist
Imaginings in Russia, 1991-2014
ISBN 978-3-8382-0665-3

131 Elisa Kriza
Alexander Solzhenitsyn: Cold War
Icon, Gulag Author, Russian
Nationalist?
A Study of the Western Reception of his
Literary Writings, Historical Interpretations,
and Political Ideas
With a foreword by Andrei Rogatchevski
ISBN 978-3-8382-0589-2 (Paperback edition)
ISBN 978-3-8382-0690-5 (Hardcover edition)

132 Serghei Golunov
The Elephant in the Room
Corruption and Cheating in Russian
Universities
ISBN 978-3-8382-0570-0

ibidem-Verlag
Melchiorstr. 15
D-70439 Stuttgart
info@ibidem-verlag.de

www.ibidem-verlag.de
www.ibidem.eu
www.edition-noema.de
www.autorenbetreuung.de